Broken Futures

Leaders and Churches Lost in Transition

Leonard Hjalmarson

Urban Loft Publishers | Skyforest, CA

Broken Futures

Leaders and Churches Lost in Transition

Urban Loft Publishers
P.O. Box 6
Skyforest, CA 92385
www.urbanloftpublishers.com

Senior Editors: Stephen Burris & Kendi Howells Douglas
Copy Editor: Frank Stirk
Graphics: Elisabeth Arnold

ISBN-13: 978-0-9989177-1-9
Made in the U.S

"Courage is the ability to cultivate a relationship with the unknown;
to create a form of friendship with what lies around
the corner over the horizon –
with those things that have not yet fully come into being…"

David Whyte

Series Preface

Urban Mission in the 21st Century is a series of monographs that addresses key issues facing those involved in urban ministry whether it be in the slums, squatter communities, favelas, or in immigrant neighborhoods. It is our goal to bring fresh ideas, a theological basis, and best practices in urban mission as we reflect on our changing urban world. The contributors to this series bring a wide-range of ideas, experiences, education, international perspectives, and insight into the study of the growing field of urban ministry. These contributions fall into four very general areas: 1—the biblical and theological basis for urban ministry; 2—best practices currently in use and anticipated in the future by urban scholar/activists who are living working and studying in the context of cities; 3—personal experiences and observations based on urban ministry as it is currently being practiced; and 4—a forward view toward where we are headed in the decades ahead in the expanding and developing field of urban mission. This series is intended for educators, graduate students, theologians, pastors, and serious students of urban ministry.

More than anything, these contributions are creative attempts to help Christians strategically and creatively think about how we can better reach our world that is now more urban than rural. We do not see theology and practice as separate and distinct. Rather, we see sound practice growing out of a healthy vibrant theology that seeks to understand God's world as it truly is as we move further into the twenty-first century. Contributors interact with the best scholarly literature available at the time of writing while making application to specific contexts in which they live and work.

Each book in the series is intended to be a thought-provoking work that represents the author's experience and perspective on urban ministry in a particular context. The editors have chosen those who bring this rich diversity of perspectives to this series. It is our hope and prayer that each book in this series will challenge, enrich, provoke, and cause the reader to dig deeper into subjects that bring the reader to a deeper understanding of our urban world and the ministry the church is called to perform in that new world.

Dr. Kendi Howells Douglas & Stephen Burris,
Urban Mission in the 21st Century Series Co-Editors

Table of Contents

List of Illustrations

Acknowledgments

Yesterday I stood in a new doorway – one I created with a hammer and a crow-bar. I first had to expose the ancient plaster and lathe on the interior wall of our hundred-year-old, and then the work began. It was messy. My right hand was beginning to ache. I was occasionally choking on dust, and it was irritating my eyes. After an hour of work, I had created a path that will be used by a generation I will never know.

The shrinking population of our churches, and the corresponding anxiety of church leaders aren't the only reasons I am writing this book. In fact, this was not the book I had intended to write. But like many good projects, the project we conceive, and the project that wants to be born are not always the same thing. As our First Nations friends like to point out, the path is made by walking.

If you intend to tread a less worn way, it's important to have wise companions. In this work, I offer one of the best companions I know: TS Eliot. Each chapter leads off with a quotation from *The Four Quartets*. Eliot shines the wisdom of the ages on the process of transition. In doing so, he normalizes the uncertainty, the paradox, and the process of endings and beginnings. In some ways this book would not have been possible without his insight.

This book invites you on a journey. I know, you've read that before. But if you race through it in a day or two, it won't yield much benefit. Take your time: consider each chapter. Bring your life and work to the text. Read contemplatively, and let the words of TS Eliot wash over you. The violence of Modernity is speed. "The space for imagination to expand is inversely proportional to the speed at which we live." (Brewin, 57) Eliot's poetry invites you into an open space; heed the call.

Broken Futures is a title and a work that embodies a paradox: in the end is our beginning. May you find hope, and wisdom, as you work through these pages.

This book grew from seeds planted by many people. Some of them are personal friends, some are acquaintances, and others I have never met. All have contributed to my life and my learning, in ways intended and unintended. They have enriched, challenged, corrected, and often humbled me by their commitment to the King of all wisdom and peace.

Thanks are due to Stan Biggs, poet and prophet and dreamer. Also to Paul Fromont, the prodigal Kiwi who so generously opened his home to me in the summer of 2016. His companionship on the journey since around 2005 has been a source of rich nourishment.

Thanks are also due to the faculty and staff in the Leadership in Global Perspectives program at Portland Seminary. They invited me to join them as an expert advisor and to participate in a learning community with leaders from around the globe.

Thanks to my wife, Elizabeth, who watched me disappear into the night to sit in front of a glowing screen. And often during daylight hours I would be distracted, staring into space pondering an elusive thought that I knew was important to the progress of this work.

Finally, thanks to Stephen Burris at Urban Loft for taking on another suddenly appearing project that failed to fit neatly into one or two popular categories! Urban Loft are a group of innovative risk-takers, dreamers who see beyond the veil to welcome the unknown future.

Foreword

By Gary Nelson
The Pace of Change is Faster than the Pace of Learning.

The Chair of our Board Steve Holmes can't remember where he first heard this statement, but it captured his imagination and thoughts. I heard it for the first time when we were discussing changes in Tyndale's strategic direction. It resonated as true and for those of us sitting around the room that day, we realized that the implications of this truth were enormous.

Nothing is sure anymore. No decision is made with an absolute guarantee of a successful outcome. There are too many variables and the conditions from which the decision is being made can be altered on the 'turn of a dime.' Changing trends, socio-political shifts and so many other influential themes can render a strategic direction obsolete even before they have been implemented.

Imagine waking up in the UK or Europe after the Brexit vote took place. How about the day after the election in the US when Donald Trump became president? Future plans which appeared so sure before these stunning surprises, are rendered irrelevant in the new setting.

It is no surprise then that leadership discussions are taking place everywhere. We wonder what leadership might look like in this time — musing on how one leads in the fast-paced complexity of a world in transition. Old definitions and strategies appear useless. Even the former assumed tool kits for effective leadership appear permanently altered in this constantly shifting environment.

For the Church and people of faith who follow Jesus, the conversation is all the more critical. We fell in love with leadership that was dynamic and hierarchical. The idea of pastoral leaders as CEO seemed to fit our egos or at least the limited leadership skills we had honed. It is difficult to give up this model, no matter how inadequate it may have been. We hold tightly to its promises and point to the places where successful implementation has taken place.

Broken Futures is written for this kind of time but calls for a different kind of leader. Len writes from a depth of praxis and theological insight that is remarkable. He synthesizes secular research on leadership but with a theological and biblical rigor that reintroduces us to an emerging understanding of leadership that is both ancient and future. If you are reading this book for a formulaic framework that enables you to lead well, then you will probably be frustrated at the end. However, if you are reading this book to build a foundational place where leadership might emerge and grow, you will find each page rich with possibilities.

Leadership at this point of history is a courageous act. It demands nimbleness, but most of all it demands value and character from which the leadership task can take place. It also demands a confident and grounded leader who can allow more than one individual to influence the process of change. The kind of leader who does not need to be 'it' and longs for others to emerge.

Almost every leadership book written in the last 20 years quotes Peter Senge. I first met Len's writings in a paper he wrote introducing this statement from Senge:

> "We are coming to believe that leaders are those people who 'walk ahead,' people who are genuinely committed to deep change in themselves and in their organizations. They lead through developing new skills, capabilities, and understandings. And they come from many places within the organization."

Leadership in the 21st century requires a social and relational IQ that stimulates collective action and engenders trust. It also demands a theological/biblical content that nurtures character and leads from values which are critical to the outcomes that might occur. Most of all, we are desperately need leaders so passionate about renewing the world that they are willing to lead differently, confidently, and from the bottom up. Broken Futures points the way ahead. You won't be disappointed.

Gary V Nelson
President, Tyndale University College & Seminary
Author, Borderland Churches and Leading in DisOrienting Times

Preface

By Michael Krause

In response to my efforts to engage seminary students with the concept of a world beyond Christendom, I see everything from knowing nods to blank stares. Some of the students have experienced the disorientation of the Postmodern context while others think that post-Christendom is just about people not coming to church anymore. I struggle to find language to express to them the massive shift that we are currently experiencing in our culture. On the one hand, I want to fan into flame their passion for God and for mission. On the other hand, I want to open their eyes to the reality that the entrenched models they rely on are from a different time and no longer communicate effectively. Are we truly in a new world where the old rules no longer apply or do we just need to try harder and be better Christians? Maybe both are true to some extent. *Broken Futures* expresses it this way: "It's difficult enough to recognize we are lost when the territory is obviously unfamiliar. How much more difficult when the familiar markers of church, home and community seem intact? Our physical environment has not changed, but our social and cultural environments are shifting like quicksand. *Are we lost, or are we not?*"

This ambiguity surfaces in different ways. We see some churches growing while others struggle to keep the doors open or to even find pastors. Certain denominations are seeing a resurgence while others are closing a church a week. Students in my classes communicate personal testimonies of encounters with God and effective ministry, while at the same time presenting case studies of dysfunctional church systems, broken relationships and oppressive leaders. So are we lost, or are we not? Hjalmarson leads us through the process of recognizing that being lost is not such a bad thing. We just need a new way of orienting ourselves. Instead of the old maps that served us well in Christendom, we need to become navigators, learning new skills so that we can navigate our way through the shifting currents of our new realities.

At the turn of the century, I planted a church – what our denomination would call an entrepreneurial church start. I was excited about what I had learned while doing some innovative work among marginalized youth in downtown Toronto and thought this innovation could be translated into a new church start-up. I was convinced that starting new churches was an effective way to evangelize and to make a difference in our communities. I had done my demographic research. I read church planting books. I attended a church-planters boot-camp. I focused my research on one of the least churched neighbourhoods in the Greater Toronto Area because I wanted to be missional. I prayed for guidance. I moved into this new neighbourhood with my young family. I prayer-walked the community. I gathered a committed and talented team to help lead the church plant. We prayed and strategized together for months. This team was committed to the vision financially. We had the support of my denomination. We sourced out a key location in a school. We communicated the vision to friends, key supporters and neighbours. We sent out fliers. We planned the first gathering event and put together a fabulous worship team. I prepared a great message. Everything was ready and we launched.

After the initial excitement, when all our friends came from far and wide to see what was going on, we settled into the reality of setting up in a school auditorium every week for only fifteen people – mostly family and team members. Why weren't we growing? I thought I had done everything right. Why was everything so wrong? The books said we should have a large stable group of people by now. What had I missed?

All the markers of success were there – at least the markers that I had come to believe were necessary for success. We were biblical. We preached the gospel. We were praying and saw answers to prayer. Worship was amazing. There was a tangible sense of the presence of God as we gathered. We reached out to our community and invited our neighbours. We advertised and communicated our vision. A number of people had made commitments to follow Jesus. We were committed to discipleship. But we weren't growing.

Looking back, I realize I had not understood how much the world had changed. However, there had been some clues. The rate of response to our mailings was minimal – about 1 contact (through a visit, phone call or email) for every 50,000 pieces sent – usually from Christians. I had some great conversations with numbers of people but not many positive responses. People seemed to like me but they didn't seem to like coming to church. The only people who did come to church were people from other churches – and they were often disgruntled, looking for something new and different. I was trying to reach non-Christians with the techniques that were attractive to Christians. I wanted to be missional in a way that was attractive to me. The path to the successful future I had imagined was laid out using a map that was printed decades earlier. Since the publication of that map, the paths had all changed. As Hjalmarson notes, "North American evangelical churches arrived at a fitness peak in the 1970s and 80s (when I attended seminary and studied those maps). In a stable and settled culture, the Christian story was accepted and even had a certain dominance, though eroding. Our impact on the culture around us was waning."

19

I had planted an innovative church service geared towards attracting Christians who were looking for one more innovation. I had planted a Sunday service not a church. The result was not a worshipping, missional community of followers of Jesus. The future I had imagined was broken. "Our cultural experience is of dislocation," says Hjalmarson. "We know that we need to find ourselves, but we aren't sure how to go about it, and our anxiety at our sense of being lost causes us to try harder, rather than to slow down and reflect. Overwhelmed by vague emotions, our brains have stopped working and we are watching for the smallest signs that the landscape might somehow be familiar. We won't find those signs, because too much has changed."

I'm wondering if this kind of failure was what I needed to get me to recognize that my vision of the future was broken. To invest everything and fail was humbling. I came to the end of my vision, to the end of my finances and to the end of myself – the dream had died. Not until I had done all that I knew how to do did I actually try something I would never have dreamed of doing when I first imagined the church plant.

I moved the church into my house.

We had gathered everyone together and said, "What do we do now?" Meeting in a house seemed to resonate with everyone. It wasn't just a prayer meeting or a Bible study. It was a house church. We stopped advertising but people who were never interested in coming to church in the school somehow found us in our house. My Jewish neighbours came to our events. They invited us to theirs. We hosted neighbourhood Christmas parties. We participated in block parties and gathered on the neighbour's lawn for Victoria Day fireworks. We became the neighbourhood hub. We increased in numbers and I had other people inviting me to help start house churches in their neighbourhoods. I felt like I had found my way again. These words from *Broken Futures* resonated with me:

The process of locating ourselves is not mystical so much as it is difficult. It is difficult because it is counter-intuitive (slowing down, not speeding up); it is communal, not individual (it requires conversation and collaboration); it feels risky (we admit we have no map); and it feels powerless (we don't know the next steps). Finding our way again is outside our control: it requires surrender to forces we don't understand. The feeling of powerlessness is a clue that this is much like a 12 step process, or a reminder that to enter the kingdom, "you must become like children.

The lessons learned in that season were transformational. I learned that I'm not in control of the church. I learned that God is not impressed with size or speed or innovation. I learned that God loves the one lost sheep and will leave the ninety-nine to go find it. I learned that God is not afraid to take the long way around if it gets us to where we should be going. I learned that God is not afraid to let something die. I learned that it's okay to experiment – and that most experiments are unsuccessful. I learned that sometimes he does some things just for me – because he loves me.

Although we remained fairly small as a house church we were able to establish a network of house churches and actually facilitate the start of another more traditional church. At one of our house church gatherings, I shared that I felt that, even though we had not grown large nor had become an "established church," my time in the house church was transformational and my transformation wouldn't have happened if we had been a more traditional church. "In some ways," I said to them, "I feel like God has done all of this just for me." To my surprise, nearly all of the other people in the room that day said they felt the same thing – God had established this church just for each of them. "I'm not lost. I'm right here!"

I wish I had found something like this book to walk with me on my journey through those years. There are a number of other books that describe the challenges the church faces in this new Postmodern and post-Christendom cultural reality. But there are few that take us by the hand in our lostness to walk us through the valley of disorientation and then out the other side. *Broken Futures* does that and helps us embrace the destabilization of our times. As I read the book I used my highlighter on phrases like "nowhere land," "edge of chaos," "too much has changed," "liminal space," "transitional places," "hinge points of history," "massive destabilization," "uncertainty rules," and "synchronous failure." Len encourages us to move through disorientation, to re-orientation and then find new forms and possibilities that emerge from the chaos. "Transition is a process of unlearning. It's painful and uncomfortable; but it's preparation to enter the unimaginable world."

Some denominations openly state that the way forward is to be more like they were in the past. While I was writing this foreword, I heard a sermon where all the illustrations were about revivals that happened a hundred years ago. The pastor's challenge to the congregation was to find our way back to the fire of those days so that God could move again. To embrace the certainty of a successful past, we were encouraged to project that passed onto our future. But that future is broken!

Those who lead churches (and those who teach seminary students) face deep challenges as we enter this new "unimaginable world." One of the theses of this book is that special demands are made of our faith communities in these transitional times. I believe one of the biggest tasks of pastors is not just to preach the gospel, nor merely disciple others. It is to participate together with their congregants to help them become "local communal theologians" who are able to discern what God is doing in their neighbourhood (their place or locality), to do it together (community) in such a way that they are able to partake in the work that the Spirit is doing around them (theology).

Broken Futures is a navigational guide that captures the journey from hope, to the end of yourself, and then back to hope again, to rediscovering the purposes of God. Hjalmarson is a synthesizer (gathering together insights from various sources and making something new) and a synergizer (making things work together in a way that is greater than the sum of the parts). Bring your highlighter and make sure you read the footnotes.

Michael Krause

Assistant Professor of Leadership

Tyndale University College and Seminary, Toronto

We shall not cease from exploration
And the end of all our exploring
Will be to arrive where we started
And know the place for the first time.

T.S. Eliot, "Little Gidding," V

Introduction

We don't need the Pew Survey or the Barna Group to tell us that we have a problem. Christian leaders are well aware of the exodus from church. Studies like those of Alan Jamieson in New Zealand and Dave Kinnaman in the USA have unveiled some of the implications of the transition we are in. While some of the mainline churches are in a kind of renewal, evangelical churches in North America are shrinking.

While the church has always been in crisis (Bosch, 1991), uncertainty and transition mark our times. We live amidst the collision of cultures and of worldviews, and the collapse of the Enlightenment synthesis. Rapid and unpredictable changes generate anxiety within us and stress within the organizations we lead. Individuals, institutions and whole communities are in transition. Reggie McNeal uses the metaphor of a violent river to describe the tension. He writes that, "Culture roils and churns in the collision of the old with the new. At the dawn of the third Christian millennium, continuity battles with discontinuity; the emergent dances with what is passing away. Leaders of spiritual enterprises, like many of the adherents of the faith, have oars in both currents. The challenge involves getting as many through the rapids as possible, knowing some will never make it." (McNeal, 2000, p. 79)

We find ourselves in a space between a liminal location, full of instability and contradictions. The old Latin word *limina* means threshold. Liminality is a space in-between where nothing seems clear. One April Sunday my family and I visited a young church community in our town. On the way to the meeting we noticed two very different restaurant signs. The first invited, "Come in from the cold; warm food and hot drinks." The second proclaimed, "Swing into spring. Escape the heat with our smoothies and Frappuccinos."

25

Is it winter, or spring? When the seasons are in transition, and the old season hasn't quite given way to the new, we don't know what kind of weather to expect or even how to dress on a given morning. When we walk out the door it might be hot, or it might be cold. Worse, it may start out warm then shift to cold while we are on the road. We are plunged into uncertainty.

When the church is in transition, the same kind of confusion surfaces. Even casual conversations can become complex, with people using language in very different ways. "Church" and "Christian" now carry baggage they didn't possess, and have different meanings relative to individual experience. The term "evangelical" once provided identity for a diverse group of believers worldwide. Now that marker itself is splintering, contested and fragile.

Liminality is emptiness and nowhere. Adolescence is the liminal space between childhood and adulthood; but what if entire communities are entering liminal space? Gareth Brandt writes, "Societal circumstances in the past few decades have created another developmental stage now known as emerging adulthood. The characteristics of this stage are inherently ambivalent, ideological, and transitional, which is why it is not easily recognizable as a distinct stage." (Brandt, 2014, p. 65). Brandt is describing a new experience of liminality that grows out of unique cultural conditions.

While Brandt applies this concept to individuals, the transition from modernity to post-modernity and from Christendom to post-Christendom, combined with the rise of new media, has generated a liminal space for *entire communities* of faith. This is a *new phase*, a new space in ecclesial life. Churches are entering a nowhere land born out of the turbulence of societal shift. We have become travelers with maps that are outdated and that no longer describe the landscape. This in turn increases our sense of lostness as well as our anxiety about the future. The higher the emotional unrest, the less likely we are to respond effectively.

General systems theory recognizes that the dynamics between individuals are mirrored on other scales. What is true for a family system can also be observed in organizational systems. In *The Critical Journey* the authors describe faith transitions as "hitting the wall." (Hagberg & Guelich, 2005, p. 12). This difficult phase, beginning with an inward journey, often occurs for individuals in mid-life. Now, however, it's happening for whole organizations. In terms of faith organizations, hitting the wall is a manifestation of liminal conditions. Churches that have hitherto been very outward oriented, busy and successful, now find themselves confronted with their deeper motivations as they begin to decline, and a thriving ministry passes into memory. The outward journey gives way to an inward journey that requires heart work and the integration of the shadow self.

In liminal space, identity is suspended. In our time we are seeing entire church families in the throes of transition: suspended in a complex dance between life and death. This transitional space generates gut-wrenching questions and tremendous insecurity. As we move into a post-Christian and post-congregational era, we seek understanding and solutions as our congregations grey and dwindle, and our ministries decline.

The Gift of Instability

Your vision will become clear only when you look into
your heart ...
Who looks outside, dreams.
Who looks inside, awakens. ~ Carl Jung, 1992, p.33.

Jung captures the paradox of the inward journey. *Who looks inside, awakens.* If liminality is an intensely uncomfortable place, it is also a place of possibility. The word "threshold" connotes a passage, a path to some-*where*. When identity is suspended, it becomes more fluid than fixed and is suddenly negotiable. But this means that liminal space is not *nowhere*, but rather is a place of possibility. If fluidity represents anti-structure to structure, it is also a place of transformation. It is a place of dying and rebirth, even of metamorphosis, the place where the caterpillar spins its cocoon and disappears from view. Liminality is Israel in the desert, Jesus in the tomb.

We know is that God is interested in transformation. Perhaps this is why liminal space is so common, and why God often engineers the journey. Few of us choose liminal space. Yet increasingly leaders and churches find themselves in these transitional places, with no markers to guide them. Richard Rohr comments that, "Nothing good or creative emerges from business as usual. This is why much of the work of God is to get people into liminal space, and to keep them there long enough so they can learn something essential. It is the ultimate teachable space . . . maybe the only one. The Jewish prophets... St. Francis, Gandhi, and John the Baptist come to mind." (Rohr, 2002, p. 9)

Is it possible that the cultural shift is serving a kingdom purpose? Is it possible that God is the designer of our present cultural transition? Yes, but perhaps not in the way we think. We might identify a cycle of birth and death and cultural renewal every 500 years or so, as Phyllis Tickle affirms in *The Great Emergence* (2008). Or we might explore adaptive science, where the church is a self-organizing system, with non-linear interactions in a changing environment, and powerful feedback loops. This implies an emergent structure more than a design, a fitting lens for an organic reality. God embedded the seeds of death and of renewal in creation itself. Living systems thrive on the edge of chaos, and begin to wither when their structures and mechanisms are too stable, their internal connections too strong.[1]

---

[1] As Gunderson puts it, "Human institutions can crash after periods of success [and] bring about their own downfall because of the stresses and rigidities that have slowly accumulated." (*Panarchy*, 2002. Kindle location 495)

Whatever interpretive framework we adopt, the challenge is the same: to rediscover God's purposes in history. What is God's invitation to us in these strange and unfamiliar places? Or, to put it in terms of the story we know so well: "How can we sing the Lord's song in a foreign land?"

Alan Roxburgh, in *The Missionary Congregation, Leadership, & Liminality*, makes the case that liminal space is hopeful, and he develops the metaphor of "spaces between." He also recognizes that the tendency in difficult times is not to dream of a new future, but instead of a familiar and idealized past. Transitions, "[place] a group in great tension. Even in complex societies the impulses of groups in the liminal state move in two directions at the same time: turning backward to recover the lost identity, and risking moving forward. Set in these terms, it is possible to locate the North American churches. Currently much of the shaping conversation is that of return. Beneath schemes of renewal and strategies of growth lie these liminal impulses of return and recovery." (Roxburgh, 1997, p. 34)

While this kind of return is a step backward, another kind of return recalls an often echoed refrain in biblical history. "Return to Me." Have our purposes been God's purposes? Did we lose sight of the kingdom of God in favor of building smaller kingdoms we could manage and control? Too much of the conversation has been about return to an idealized past. That conversation merely increases how stuck we are and prevents rich engagement and fresh listening to God in our current location. Trying to return to an idealized "glory days" prevents an *adaptive* response.

In General Systems Theory, *homeostasis* describes the resistance of a system to change, and its tendency to seek stability. But a system that is pushed beyond its ability to adapt or compensate must seek a new basis of stability. Biologists use the term *fitness* to describe the ability of an organism to adapt to changing conditions. Fitness depends on numerous interrelated factors and is a complex mechanism that recognizes non-linearity and even chaos.

While the hope is that organizations and individuals can successfully navigate complex conditions and come out the other side stronger, one only has to look around to see that this is not always the case. When we feel overwhelmed, we tend to bury our heads in the sand or try harder, looking for a bigger hammer. Ronald Wright, in examining Mayan civilization, has demonstrated that civilizations near the end of their life-cycle increase their pace as they sense that the party is nearly over, ensuring their rapid collapse. (Wright, 2004, p. 102).

What we need are alternatives. When we move beyond familiar spaces, our previous experience may constrain rather than enable us. Eugene Lowry writes, "The reason that flashes of insight come when one is not looking is that our cognitive ruts lose their tenacious hold upon us when our mind is occupied with other things or begins to drift as we go to sleep. Hence, the unthinkable thought (generally inverted from common sense) has a chance to break through. Such uncommon sense comes as an intuitive, 'aha!'" (Lowry, 2001, p. 53).

Unfortunately, the more we know about a subject, the more apt we are to stay locked into our assumptions, and hence become blind to alternative perspectives.

In Luke 9 and 10 Jesus offers us good advice for entering unknown places and discovering a new future. He recommends that we "take nothing for the journey." Wait a minute: take *nothing* with us? It's counter-intuitive. We are trained to be prepared; to make our best forecast of what lies ahead so that we are pre-adapted to the expected conditions. The trouble is, our preferred future is usually only the past projected forward.

Laurence Gonzales in *Deep Survival* describes exactly that response, and tells story after story of explorers and mountaineers who thought they were prepared, only to discover that they were sabotaged by their expectations of the future. We prepare for what we know, based on our experience of the past.

How then do we let go of our assumptions, even of our need to succeed? How do we become truly open to a new context and new learning? How do we enter an open space and dwell there? How do we, like Jesus, "empty ourselves" and become nothing? The lesson of Philippians 2 is humility – the need of a deeper spirituality. But how do we go deeper when we are fearful of letting go? The paradox of surrender invites us to a new journey, a renewed pilgrimage. As Lao Tzu has aptly noted, "a good traveler has no fixed plans, and is not intent on arriving."

Thankfully, we have guides who through the centuries have gone before us, entering into the paradox of pilgrimage, getting beyond the polarities of movement and stability. TS Eliot is one such guide, who invites us to know the end in our beginning. As we move through these chapters – an inner journey into an open space – we'll consider the strange realities of our time, consider the nature of adaptive challenge, examine new metaphors for leadership and change, and close with thoughts on renewed engagement in the strange and complex world we inhabit.

Questions are fateful. They determine destinations. They are the chamber through which destiny calls.

Godwin Hlatshwayo (2008)

CHAPTER 1

Systems in Transition

In 2014 Canadian explorers made a magnificent discovery, locating one of the two Franklin expedition ships in the high Arctic. The history is well known. Captain Sir John Franklin left England in 1845 on two ships with a crew of 128 officers and men in search of the Northwest Passage to the Pacific Ocean. It was a great adventure, in an age of adventure and discovery.

The crew knew they were heading out into unknown waters on a journey of discovery; they knew there were risks. Not one member of the crew was ever found alive again. Their bodies have now been found in shallow graves, dispersed across the frozen Arctic. *What happened?*

It wasn't an ordinary expedition. The ships, *Erebus* and *Terror*, were specially constructed. They were technological marvels of the age. And the ships and crews were already veterans: they had taken a successful four-year mission to Antarctica, charting much of that continent's coastline under the leadership of Captain James Ross.

The ships were triple-masted. Their bows were reinforced with iron sheets to deflect polar ice, and full-sized steam engines added horsepower via a screw propeller. Beneath their decks, the *Erebus* and *Terror* carried copious rations. The manifest listed 24 tons of meat, 35 tons of flour, nearly two tons of tobacco, and no less than 7,500 liters of liquor. This was meant to sustain the 128-man crew for three full years, but the expedition didn't endure that long.

What happened?

A hint is found in how the expedition provisioned itself, what they saw as *necessary* for the journey. Franklin was a careful man and a scientist. He understood something of the challenges that lay ahead, in a time when old ways of understanding the world were falling and a new world was emerging. He would also have talked with those few other men who had sailed up to the Arctic, seeking to learn from their experience. *But in spite of this – they all died!* Alan Roxburgh writes that, "The [ship's] manifest tells us what these adventurers *understood* to be important --and necessary for the journey. It captures the world in which they lived, a way of understanding themselves and their world. And that tradition would destroy them, because it made little sense in the environment of the Arctic." (Roxburgh, 2008)

Franklin equipped his ships with a 1200-volume library; a hand organ that played fifty tunes; china place settings and expensive silver flatware. These Victorian-era Englishmen *took their world* with them.

So important were these elements of their normal life in England that they only carried a *twelve day supply* of coal for their auxiliary engines, yet knowing the journey would last two to three years. Roxburgh continues,

> The habits and customs of their world determined what they took with them when they abandoned ship to seek help. Bodies were found lying out on the frozen ice or in shallow graves, with their silver beside them. Despite their brave commitment to explore a new way through the North West Passage, Franklin and his crew went with the assumptions of a 19th Century English world. Those assumptions, based on their previous lives, killed them in the new space they entered. (Roxburgh, 2008)

Franklin's story is a metaphor for what is happening to churches today. The programs we bring with us to innovate for tomorrow are like the china plates and library books that shaped the imagination of Franklin. They don't help us create a new world: *they only prevent us from leaving the familiar past behind.* They provide the sense of safety that prevents rich engagement in a new location.

Our old future is broken, and often just the familiar past is projected forward, not a true future at all. *How do we walk with God into a new future – an unknown place?*

Complexity and the Adaptive Challenge

If turbulent waters signal cultural shift, the confluence of other streams promises new insight into the nature of the change itself. Complexity science grapples with the nature of life and change, and is the combination of three streams: 1) breakthroughs in life sciences, particularly biology and ecology; 2) new data in social science, particularly economics and psychology; and 3) new discoveries in the hard sciences, particularly physics, math, and information technologies. But how do these disciplines help us to navigate the complex waters of cultural shift?

Over the past twenty or thirty years, a new body of literature has emerged around the science of complexity. This is a broad enquiry into the common properties of living things – beehives and bond traders, ecologies and economies. These insights have more recently been applied to human organizations, and have begun to impact management and business models, helping us understand confusing networks of interaction. For the purpose of this study, we need to consider four principles that grow out of the science of complexity that apply to the living system we call church. These principles are:

1. Equilibrium is a precursor to death. When a living system is in a stable state, it is less responsive to changes occurring around it. This places it at high risk.

2. In the face of threat, or when galvanized by a compelling opportunity, living things move to the *edge of chaos*. This unstable condition evokes innovation and novelty, and fresh solutions are more likely to be found.

3. When this destabilization occurs, the components of a living system *self-organize* and new forms and possibilities emerge from the chaos.

4. Living systems cannot be *directed* along a linear path. Unanticipated consequences are inevitable. The challenge is to disturb the system in such a way that the desired outcome is more likely. (Pascale, Millemann, Gioja, 2000, p. 6)

Lawrence Miller in his 1990 book *Barbarians to Bureaucrats*, notes that organizations have definable life-cycles and pass through predictable stages from life to death and sometimes to rebirth (Miller, 1990). As Jean Vanier put it, what begins in passion often ends in bureaucracy, with ways and means becoming set in cement, and often continuing to run long after the purpose is forgotten. A system like this is no longer responsive to its environment, and inevitably a collapse follows. New life springs from the decaying remains of the old. The following illustration is based in part on the work of Joseph Schumpeter and is found in *Panarchy: Understanding Transformations in Human and Natural Systems*.

Figure 1

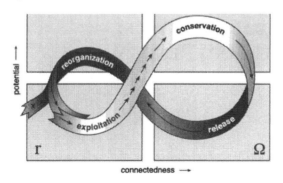

37

There are four phases in the adaptive cycle, and here I follow the description offered in *Panarchy*, by Lance H. Gunderson.

1. The rapid growth or *r* phase. Early in the cycle, the system is engaged in a period of rapid growth, as actors colonize recently disturbed areas. These species (referred to as r-strategists in ecosystems), utilize disorganized resources to exploit an ecological niche. They are start-ups and producers of new products; they capture shares in newly opened markets – such as new churches in new suburbs!

2. The conservation or K phase. During this phase, energy and materials slowly accumulate. Connections between the actors increase. The competitive edge shifts from species that adapt well to external variability and uncertainty to those that reduce the impact of a changing environment through their own mutually reinforcing relationships. The growth rate slows as connectedness increases to the point of rigidity: resilience declines. Such a system is increasingly stable, but over a decreasing range of conditions. "People want to stabilize [churches] for economic purposes. By doing that, we tend to lower the resilience of systems." (Gunderson, 2012, Kindle Location 188)

3. The release or omega (Ω) phase. A disturbance that exceeds the system's resilience breaks apart its web of reinforcing interactions. This could be the loss of a founding pastor, or a sudden decline in employment in the area, or increased competition for members, or a major shift in demographics. In an abrupt turnabout, the material and energy accumulated during the conservation phase is released. Resources that were

tightly bound are transformed or destroyed as connections break and systemic controls weaken. The release of accumulations of resources generates a creative element.

4. The renewal or alpha (α) phase. Following a disturbance, uncertainty rules. Feeble internal controls allow a system to lose or gain resources, but also allow novelty to appear. Small, chance events have the opportunity to powerfully shape the future. Invention, experimentation, and re-assortment are the rule. In ecosystems, pioneer species may appear from previously suppressed vegetation; seeds germinate; non-native plants can invade and dominate the system. Skills, experience, and expertise lost by individual groups may coalesce around new opportunities. Novelty arises in the form of new initiatives, creative ideas, and new people. (Gunderson, 2012, Kindle Locations 167-176)

An example of the adaptive cycle is offered in *Panarchy*, based on a classic ecological study of spruce/fir forests that grow across a huge swath of North America. Among the forests' many inhabitants is the spruce budworm, a moth whose larvae eat the new green needles on coniferous trees. Every 40 to 120 years, populations of spruce budworm explode, killing off up to 80 per cent of the balsam firs. But what looks like destruction turns out to be necessary for the health of the system. Renewal follows this episode as nutrients are released, and the forests regrow to repeat the cycle.

Following World War II, before the dynamics of the system were understood, a campaign to control spruce budworm became a huge effort to regulate a natural resource using pesticide spraying. The attempt was to minimize the economic consequences of the pest on the forest industry in Eastern Canada. It ran into problems early on. "The goal was not to eliminate the insect but to keep the forest green, which, unfortunately, is good for budworm too, since they like mature trees" (Gunderson, 2012, Kindle Location 222). While the spraying regime avoided a catastrophic outbreak, it allowed the insect to flourish while the problem spread. Meanwhile, the limited success of the program had other consequences, increasing industry's dependence on the spraying program, and spawning more pulp mills.

Ecosystem management generally focuses on maximizing the output of a particular product with the goal of increasing productivity of a narrowly defined product. A very similar story is offered from the corporate world in the development of the first arterial stent by Johnson & Johnson in 1994. (Pascale, Millemann, Gioja, 2000, p. 171-174). These efforts at control reduce the overall resilience of the system, leaving it rigid and vulnerable. At the same time, management becomes myopic and rigid, focused on maximizing success. Related industries become more dependent and inflexible.

Consider the North American church: our goal (product) is disciples. We have focused on maximizing output, but we have done this mostly by aiming our effort at getting butts in seats. We have largely assumed that the more people who attend our services, the greater will be our output of disciples. But as REVEAL demonstrated, this has not been the case (Christianity Today, 2008).

Meanwhile the *perception* of success, a full house in a large auditorium, and abundant finances as a result, has been a powerful incentive to keep doing more of the same. Leaders become myopic, fixated on maintaining the methods that attract large crowds. The system becomes rigid, finely tuned toward the goal of keeping the place full and the wheels turning. The stronger the element of design, the less often we see novelty and adaptation to a changing environment. As Gunderson notes, "Human institutions can crash after periods of success [and] bring about their own downfall because of the stresses and rigidities that have slowly accumulated." (Gunderson, *Ibid.*) Kevin Kelly of *Wired Magazine* wrote that, "Organizations, like living beings, are hardwired to optimize what they know and not to throw success away. A company expends energy to move its butt uphill, or to evolve its product so that it is sitting on top, where it is maximally adapted to the consumer environment. Companies find devolving (a) unthinkable and (b) impossible." (Kelly, 1997, p. 192-194)

The resulting problem is thus twofold: 1) we are not producing disciples, but rather consumers. Any attempt to switch focus results (as it should!) in a crisis; 2) the system we have produced is self-referenced and largely a closed loop, out of touch with the surrounding culture. Thus, we can't quickly change tracks to engage those who need the gospel because we lack the local knowledge needed to connect with them. Moreover, the most creative leaders are often among those who have already left the building, tired of the limits on their creativity and tired of seeking to be heard by those too busy to listen. The loss of these creative types only hastens the systemic decline.

The New Environment

In this fallen world, success both potentiates and creates inevitable problems. Humans thrive on stability – but the gospel seems to thrive on the edge of chaos. That produces an inherent tension in our organizations. But note that the cycle we are seeing is *designed into* living systems; it's in the DNA. This means that the current decline we are seeing may be a naturally occurring phenomenon, not something sovereignly engineered by God, though God will use it to equip his people for mission and to purify our motives.

A comment on emergence and design is in order here. Emergence and design exist on a continuum – a system drifting too far toward design becomes rigid, and will have difficulty generating new experiments when adaptation is necessary. On the other hand, a system moving too far toward emergence will have difficulty delivering its products and growing as an organism. Engineer types love to design structures; artistic types constantly tear them down, hoping something new will emerge. We need some structures in order to grow an organization and generate some predictability. But too much structure results in rigidity and over-management, which saps creativity.

While the problems and challenges are real, and evangelical churches are shrinking in Western settings, there are still signs of life in the West. In Canada this is documented in video productions like *One Size Fits All* (Joe Manafo) and in books like *Borderland Churches* (2008) and *Text & Context* (2013). The Downtown Windsor Community Collaborative in Windsor, Ontario, is rediscovering the power of community and collaboration for the common good. The Journey Network in Ottawa, Ontario, is rediscovering parish even as they decentralize the function of leadership. Metro Community in Kelowna, B.C. has moved back into the downtown core and thrives in their ministry to the poor and marginalized. Calvary Grandview Baptist in Vancouver, B.C. moved from a commuter church to a parish church working for justice while deepening connections in their neighbourhood.

These shifts are occurring around the globe, in Capetown, Auckland, Hong-Kong, London, San Francisco and Denver. Agencies empowering leaders to fresh engagement are likewise emerging. In the UK and Australia there are FORGE and Fresh Expressions, now both active in North America. Also in the UK documents like "Mission Shaped Church" (2003) have grown out of serious attempts to understand cultural shift and re-engage. In the USA and Canada, The Gospel and our Culture Network was formed in the mid 1980s, resulting in many reflective articles as well as *Missional Church* (Jossey-Bass, 1998). More recently Ryan Bolger edited *The Gospel After Christendom* (Baker, 2012), relating stories of innovation and renewal from around the world. Around the same time the Parish Network was growing legs in B.C., Washington and Oregon. Unfortunately, our educational institutions lag behind and often continue to train leaders for a stable Christendom culture.

Navigators, not Map Readers

In a crisis, we call for someone with answers, decision, strength, and a map of the future — in short, someone who can make hard problems simple. But instead of looking for saviours, we should be calling for leadership that will challenge us to face problems for which there are no simple, painless solutions   problems that require us to learn new ways. (Heifetz, 1994, p. 21).

In the spring of 1980 I was looking for a job. I crossed paths with a college friend who had secured a summer job as a fishing guide, and I headed with him up to Stuart Island, in the mouth of Bute Inlet.

My first day of training was eye-opening. I thought the ocean was a large, predictable body of water. I found myself being pushed around in a small boat in tidal waters between islands. Imagine a river that flows north one day at four knots. The next morning you return to the same place and it's flowing south at six knots. Huge whirlpools spin off rocks, sometimes reaching two hundred feet across and fifty feet in depth. Change is constant. The "terrain" of the ocean and its currents are unpredictable because of islands, underwater obstacles, and the weather. While the phases of the moon offered us a guideline in terms of the time of maximum flow, even maximum flow varied by a knot or more depending on location.

We live in a time where the landscape has become fluid. What was once predictable and stable is now like the rapids I faced as a sport fishing guide: one day 4 knots south, the next day 6 knots north. Like the chaos of tidal waters, the settled and predictable ways of Modernity and Christendom have given way to plurality and fragmentation.

What do we do when maps no longer describe the territory? How do we locate ourselves, and then find the way forward? Eddie Gibbs offers the clue: when maps stop working, we train navigators.

The Church needs navigators tuned to the voice of God, not map-readers. Navigational skills have to be learned on the high seas and in the midst of varying conditions produced by the wind, waves, currents, fogbanks, darkness, storm clouds and perilous rocks (Gibbs, 2005, p. 66).

Navigation is a significantly different skill than map reading. The points on a map are fixed, and when one wants to travel in the real world one simply locates oneself by correspondence to known geography or artifacts, and then proceeds step by step to the next point. If you have a compass and a bit of logic, this is really, really easy.

But *navigation* requires no fixed planetary points. Instead, one learns to read the sky – the stars, really – and orients oneself by a point *outside* the world. This requires a sense of 3D space, and the ability to apply an *imaginative framework* to the real world.

Map reading requires only logic and a table top. Any ten-year-old can master it then take a compass and use that knowledge with a high degree of confidence. Navigation, on the other hand, is a skill that is learned in the wilderness or on the ocean. It requires courage and the ability to withstand harsh conditions. When we can't reference earthly artefacts we need something outside the world: the North Star.

Navigation is both an old skill and an ancient metaphor. John Climacus used the Greek work *kubernetes* in his early seventh-century book *Ladder of Divine Ascent*. The word means *pilot, helmsman, or guide*, and he used it to speak of spiritual direction. When a ship is entering a harbour universal knowledge is no longer adequate; local knowledge becomes critical. The pilot comes alongside the captain and crew to guide them safely through unfamiliar waters, past hidden obstacles. Travelling in a straight line in unknown waters can get you killed.

Navigators need something that is never required of map readers: faith and a fundamental inner quiet. When there are no physical points by which to locate ourselves, our emotional brain takes over and we stop thinking. Navigators require internal self-controls that map readers don't need.

We don't really need navigators in times of cultural stability; we need them desperately in seasons of transition. And as we might expect, we have great stories of navigators in the Old Testament. There were no maps for the people of Israel leaving Egypt, only a cloud by day and a pillar of fire by night.

Journeys off the Map

Most of us began our journey in leadership with a clear sense of purpose, and a decent set of skills and capacities. We trained in a context that had a clear and set agenda, to prepare us for another context that was predictable and stable. If we were lucky, we then found a job in an organization that was also fairly stable, and we experienced a satisfying measure of success. That experience bolstered our sense of self, and we settled into a rhythm that we expected would continue until retirement. And then everything went south.

When the environment is stable, as we observed above, we get used to rhythms and routines that don't offer much challenge. We know how to work the system and achieve our goals. The organization grows and our skillset grows and expands. And then something unexpected happens. The context changes. We lose key leaders to age, movement, burn-out, or a host of other factors. Perhaps there is a major church battle. Whatever the reason, it becomes more and more difficult to just maintain stability, much less grow the organization. This experience of "hitting the wall" may be very personal, or it may seem to occur outside of us. No matter, the result is the same. We find ourselves asking uncomfortable questions about our vocation, our identity, and about God's purposes in our work. Suddenly the outward journey becomes an inward journey.

It's tough enough when this happens to individuals. But now entire churches have entered a nowhere land that has come into being in the turbulent waters of societal shift. We have become travelers with maps that are outdated and that no longer describe the landscape. Complex cultural forces are now generating liminal space for entire communities of people.

When churches hit the wall the level of anxiety can be extremely high. Leaders in particular feel enormous pressure to develop a plan that will effectively move the community forward to a new experience of stability, if not growth. But frequently leaders lack both the knowledge and the skill to embark on the necessary journey. The old maps have failed and the knowledge needed for navigation on a turbulent ocean has not been developed.

Organizations are optimized for success in a narrow environmental range. When the environment shifts drastically, we barely know where to start. Moreover, the creative and innovative types typically found other challenges and moved on. We lack even the resources to begin to engage in the new space we are in. Can we admit we are lost and don't know where to begin? Can we learn to listen for the unknown future? Can we trust that God will lead us forward as we move off the map?

One voice tells us to work harder; another blames the context. If we just had different skills, more help, a younger organization, etc., then we could find our way through. Another voice, buried by the anxious voice on the surface, is more authentic. It calls us to be still, to trust and wait on God. It tells us that the answer we seek is not the latest program for church growth but something more obvious that has been there all along. We somehow know there is a new future ahead of us, but the wall that stops us seems overwhelming. We feel like David facing Goliath but without a slingshot!

If we are wise enough to pay attention to the quieter voice, it might sound something like this:
Enough.
These few words are enough.
If not these words, this breath.
If not this breath, this sitting here.
This opening to the life

we have refused
again and again
until now.
Until now. (Whyte, 2002, p. 256)

What if everything in your life was actually enough? We don't usually consider this possibility. What if you could claim this strange and painful place as a gift?

In *The Present Future* Reggie McNeal offers this word for tired leaders:

"God must have a lot of confidence in you to put you on the planet at just this time. It was his sovereign decision to insert you onto planet earth during a time of huge transition. It takes incredible faith to lead during hinge points of history.

"Think about John the Baptist as a transitional leader. John saw heaven open and the Spirit descend when he baptized his first cousin. Yet when he was in jail he sent word to Jesus, "Now, let's go over this one more time: are you the one?" Jesus doesn't slam John. In fact, he extols his cousin: "There's never been a better man born," Jesus says (Luke 7:28).

"Jesus doesn't slam you for your doubts, fears and uncertainties either. He wants to encourage you in your current assignment. You are being asked to lead during a time when you are not sure where all this is going . . . You are leading by faith, trusting that the subplot obediences you practice will contribute to the larger drama. Your courage to believe with partial sight will be rewarded one day when a full view is afforded.

"On the flip side, you have the chance to do what only a few have been privileged to do. You get the chance to give shape to the movement that will define its expression for perhaps hundreds of years (if Jesus tarries). You must choose carefully." (McNeal, 2003, p. 120)

At the center of your experience is God and his grace. Place your trust in him as you work toward understanding this awkward place we are in. The experience of feeling lost is just that: an experience. You aren't lost. *You are right here.*

I said to my soul, be still, and wait without hope
For hope would be hope for the wrong thing; wait without love,
For love would be love of the wrong thing; there is yet faith
But the faith and the love and the hope are all in the waiting.

TS Eliot, Four Quartets. "East Coker, III"

CHAPTER 2

Getting Lost

Ken Killip set out on a trail in Rocky Mountain National Park at
dawn on August 8, 1998. He had the feeling that he should not have
come. He had plenty of outdoor experience. He had been with the
Parker Fire Protection District just south of Denver for twenty-four
years. He'd even had some survival training in the military. But Killip
had never seen terrain so rugged and it plus the altitude, and the heavy
pack were taking a toll.

Killip had been following his friend York, who had been there
before and who knew the way. While Killip had the map, York had the
compass. They had started on the trail, but beyond the top of Mount
Ida, it was a trail-less wilderness where both map and compass are
recommended. As Killip watched York pull further ahead then
disappear into the gathering storm, he didn't realize the danger he was
in.

When we enter unfamiliar territory we quickly form a mental
model: an internal set of directions and markers that describe an area.
Killip had a sense of where he was in relation to the starting point and
his car, but since following York he had not been checking the
topographical map, so his mental map was not updated in relation to the

route and the rugged terrain. Now his brain was attempting to coordinate the route from a position he did not know to a destination he had not seen. And furthermore, a storm was rolling in. He decided to wait on the slope below the ridge until the storm passed, and was soon joined by some day-hikers who came off the trail. When the lightning finally stopped, Killip pressed on in a driving rain, hoping to salvage the trip. He was climbing a steep slope he was sure must be Mount Ida, though in fact it was not.

Killip was tired; he had been walking all day with a heavy pack. He was uncomfortable and carried a sense of anxiety: partly the disorientation of the storm, partly an awareness that he was working off a hazy model of his location. But he pictured himself on Mount Ida and that gave him a sense of comfort. He'd been in motion for more than twelve hours and had drunk the last of his water three hours before. The sun was going down and the temperature was dropping.

When Killip finally struggled to the top, he turned east and began the descent into the drainage, following his internal sense of where Rock Lake should be. But he immediately knew something was wrong. The river and the little lakes that York had described were not there. His internal image and the real world did not match. His anxiety increased. Killip teetered on the brink of two worlds: his confusion was minor and he could have retraced his steps. He knew what was behind him; he did not know what was ahead. He had lost the vital ability to perceive the real world and therefore perceive his own future.

Laurence Gonzales relates this story in his book *Deep Survival: Who Lives, Who Dies and Why* (Gonzales, 2003). Psychologists who study the behaviour of people who get lost report that few ever backtrack. Instead, they look forward into their *imagined* world, the world in which they know where they are and where they are in control. But as the stress on the brain increases, its ability to reason is degraded in favor of emotional controls. Dislocation degenerates into panic.

Until a century ago scientists believed that people had an inherent sense of direction. Observations of more primitive tribes seemed to support this, until researchers realized that primitive people are trained from childhood to pick up very subtle cues from the environment and use them to find a route. And even primitive people still get lost. The ones who do not are operating from an up-to-date mental map of the geography.

Eventually Killip found himself blundering through dense timber in total darkness with the feeling he was nowhere. He finally settled down near a pond where he could drink. He could have built a fire but he knew open fires weren't permitted in the area. He was able to heat a meal on his camp stove and then fell asleep. When he awoke he felt somewhat refreshed. He could have retraced his steps to his car, but he felt he couldn't abandon York, and anyway, he didn't *quite* believe he was lost.

Admitting you are lost is the most difficult part of the experience, because having no mental map, being no place, is like having no *self*. It's impossible to conceive, because one of the main jobs of our brain is to adjust itself to place. Eventually Killip was bushwhacking through forest so dense he sometimes had to remove his pack to squeeze between trees. This was a bad sign, but there was too much adrenalin in his system for him to recognize it. William Syrotuck writes, "If things get progressively more unfamiliar and mixed up, [the victim] may then develop a feeling of vertigo, the trees and the slopes seem to be closing in and a feeling of claustrophobia compels them to try to 'break out.' This is the point at which running or frantic scrambling may occur," as the brain desperately tries to get a fix on a strange environment. (Syrotuck, 2000, p. 160).

Killip's case and his behaviours are not unusual, and actually fit a pattern. Gonzales identifies some predictable behaviors of lost people.

1. People who are lost at first deny they're lost. They're confident that they know where they are, they just can't find any familiar signs. Everything's okay, they still know where they're going, the maps are still correct. Gradually confronted with strange and unfamiliar sights, anxiety creeps in. They speed up their activity, urgently wanting to verify that they're not lost. Those lost on a mountain walk faster or go in circles; those lost in a failing organization work longer, harder, and go in circles.

2. At this point, doubt and uncertainty creep in. People become angry and impatient, pushing aside any information that doesn't confirm their location. They become desperate to find any bit of information that proves they know where they are. They reject all other data, and treat as enemy the information or messenger that would help them get unlost.

3. When this strategy fails, people realize they can no longer deny that they're lost. Fear and panic set in, and their brains stop working. Now every action they take is senseless, creating more fatigue and more problems.

4. Confused and panicked, people search frantically for any sign that's familiar. But they *are* lost, so this strategy fails and they continue to deteriorate.

It's difficult enough to recognize we are lost when the territory is obviously unfamiliar. How much more difficult when the familiar markers of church, home and community seem intact? Our physical environment has not changed, but our social and cultural environments are shifting like quicksand. *Are we lost, or are we not?* People lost in the wilderness, whose immediate survival is at stake, have only one option left. They must accept their situation: they are truly lost. Gonzales writes, "Like it or not, you must make a new mental map of where you are or you will die. To survive, you must find yourself. Then it won't matter where you are. Not being lost is not a matter of getting back to where you started from; it is a decision not to be lost wherever you happen to find yourself. It's simply saying, 'I'm not lost, I'm right here.'" (Gonzales, 2003, p. 180)

Lost? I'm Right Here

Lost was an American drama television series that launched in 2004, following the lives of the survivors of a plane crash on a mysterious tropical island. There, they had to negotiate an unknown monster, an unpredictable group of prior occupants, strange, other-worldly island inhabitants and each other as they tried to survive and attract rescue. Lost was filmed on location in Hawaii, and co-creator Damon Lindelof commented that, "This show is about people who are metaphorically lost in their lives, who get on an airplane, and crash on an island, and become physically lost on the planet Earth. And once they are able to metaphorically find themselves in their lives again, they will be able to physically find themselves in the world again." (Goldman, 2007).

The story that was *Lost* gripped the public in Canada and the USA because our cultural experience is of dislocation. We know that we need to find ourselves, but we aren't sure how to go about it, and our anxiety at our sense of being lost causes us to try harder, rather than to slow down and reflect. Overwhelmed by vague emotions, our brains have stopped working and we are watching for the smallest signs that the landscape might somehow be familiar. *We won't find those signs*, because too much has changed.

The process of locating ourselves is not so much mystical as it is difficult. It is difficult because it is counter-intuitive (slowing down, not speeding up); it is communal, not individual (it requires conversation and collaboration); it feels risky (we admit we have no map); and it feels powerless (we don't know the next steps). Finding our way again is outside our control: it requires surrendering to forces we don't understand. The feeling of powerlessness is a clue that this is much like

55

a twelve-step process, or a reminder that to enter the kingdom, "you must become like children" (Matt 18:3).

When complex systems are disturbed they move rapidly from equilibrium to disequilibrium, to the edge of chaos. As they seek for a new stability, they move toward what are called "strange attractors," a phenomenon physicists and biologists both describe in adaptive systems, and which are experientially similar to serendipity.

The process itself is akin to emergence, and involves several stages. A triggering event is generated and them amplified by feedback loops, a network of communications. This could be a random comment that the church down the road is experiencing remarkable growth. Or it might be the opposite: the news that most churches in our denomination are in decline. Or it could be the brain finally recognizing that we *are well and truly lost.*

The next stage is instability, and it is experienced as tension, chaos, confusion, self-doubt or pain, and can be experienced as an existential crisis. This was how atomic scientists described their work in the 1920s, when their explorations brought them into contact with a strange new reality. They rapidly became aware that their basic concepts, their language, and their whole mental map of reality were inadequate. Werner Heisenberg described this period as an emotional crisis: "I remember discussions with Bohr which went through many hours till very late at night and ended almost in despair; and when at the end of the discussion I went alone for a walk in the park I repeated to myself again and again the question: can nature possibly be so absurd as it seemed to us in these atomic experiments?" (Capra, 2002, p. 118)

While not all experiences of transition are so extreme, they commonly involve a sense of uncertainty and loss of control. The challenge for leaders through these times is to promote a climate of trust and openness so that the knowledge-sharing required to explore new territory is not neglected.

In the previous chapter we noted that systems that are stable for too long lose their resilience, their ability to adapt to new conditions. In our new social location conditions change so rapidly that the metaphor that best fits our times is *fluidity*. Where once we could rely on a slow and predictable rate of change, and familiar effects following predictably from familiar causes, the conditions of our time are constantly in flux, connected in ways we don't understand, and indeterminate in nature. These conditions are *fluid.*

'Fluidity' is the quality of liquids and gases. They exist in an in-between state that is a phase transition. While solids have clear spatial dimensions, fluids do not keep to any shape and are prone to change it. And they neither fix space nor bind time. Zygmunt Bauman notes that "when describing solids, one may ignore time altogether; in describing fluids, to leave time out of the account would be a grievous mistake. Descriptions of fluids are all snapshots, and they need a date at the bottom of the picture." (Bauman, 2000, p. 2).

The point Bauman is making is that change in our time has become the constant. The qualities of our time, including the institutions themselves, have become fluid. He notes that the first solids to be melted in modernity were traditional loyalties, customary rights and obligations. Liquidity is now a prime characteristic of the economic, cultural and intellectual forces of our era. Meaning, identity, gender roles and social life, including a sense of rootedness in place, were once fixed qualities. But in recent decades these solids have melted at a pace that rivals that of the failing Greenland glaciers.

Fluidity and Context

This fluidity now lies at the core of our culture; our entire world is in transition. The liminality we experience in our churches is a manifestation of liminality in the larger culture. Oddly, this isn't as gloomy as it sounds. The properties of liquid are emergent, and emergent properties produce emergent behaviour. (Waldrop, 1992, p. 82). If our organizations are in a transition phase, then we know two

things: *they are not what they were, and not yet what they will become.*
Instead of expending useless energy attempting to make a liquid into a
solid, instead of attempting to halt the transition and force a new
stability, we have to learn to trust the God who works mysteriously in
history, and who delights to give us his kingdom. We have to learn to
wait.

In *The Upside of Down* Thomas Homer-Dixon contends that five
"tectonic stresses" are accumulating deep underneath the surface of
today's global order. Taken together, these stresses greatly increase the
risk of a cascading collapse of systems vital to our well-being, a
phenomenon he calls "synchronous failure." That's gloomy! So what is
the "up" side? Homer-Dixon writes, "We can get ready in advance to
turn to our advantage any breakdown that does occur... We can boost
the chances that it will lead to renewal by being well prepared, nimble
and smart and by learning to recognize its many warning signs."
(Homer-Dixon, 2007, p. 21). Elsewhere he uses a word for the process of
renewal that comes through breakdown: *catagenesis.* It describes a
process that results when complex systems adapt to new conditions.

After a prolonged immersion in uncertainty and doubt, the
discovery of new solutions or a new equilibrium can feel like a miracle.
Artists and scientists both describe these moments of awe and wonder
when a confused situation suddenly resolves into a new idea or a new
state of reality. Since this arrival is usually through nonlinear means, it
can be difficult to describe. It doesn't lend itself to clear analysis and
can't be explained in conventional language. These same qualities also
make local solutions very difficult to transfer laterally to other locations.
Emergent solutions are generated in *local cultures*, and while principles
may sometimes transfer, the solution itself does not. (We'll consider
context in some detail in chapter 5.)

When Tim Dickau arrived at Grandview Calvary Baptist Church
in Vancouver in 1989, the church had already been in decline for ten
years. A once thriving community, around seventy people continued to

call the church their home. The context had changed dramatically over 25 years; it had become multi-cultural while the church had remained mono-cultural. They had grown insular and inward, people were leaving the community for the suburbs, and there was no clear sense of call to be the church where they were. Only twenty of those who remained lived in the immediate neighbourhood. Moreover, dualisms of Sunday and Saturday, church and community, prevailed.

The apparent "stability" of Grandview in 1990 was a deathly stability, fixed and complacent. It was critical to move to a more fluid state, away from stability, and begin to re-enter the neighbourhood and adapt to the changed context. Slowly and intentionally, over six to seven years, the church grew and turned a corner, becoming a diverse community of people on mission together, re-discovering the meaning of *parish*. Committed families began to intentionally move into the neighbourhood to further the work there.

In order to make this new beginning, some things had to end. Gone were the days of waiting for someone else to be the missionary. Gone were the days when things were the same from day to day and from Sunday to Sunday. Gone were the days when everything was predictable, and the cultural norms for faith were determined by a white, middle class majority. Things began to change, and as Tim recalls those days he remembers the sense of vulnerability and the uncertainty of the journey. (Dickens, 2015)

Endings and Beginnings

Henry Cloud in *Necessary Endings* writes of the things that prevent us from making new beginnings. The problem with beginnings is that they require endings, and not many of us are good at endings. (Cloud, 2010).

The reasons we are bad at endings are varied and complex. Some of us have acquired a learned helplessness, where when things are going very badly we let negative self-talk dominate our minds. When faced with a need to make a change, we adapt to the misery. We convince ourselves that it's totally outside our control. Perhaps we have a victim mentality. In reality, we nearly always have options.

Many of us passionately avoid endings, and others avoid certain *kinds* of endings. We avoid endings because we have an internal map, or internal software, that tells us that certain endings are wrong. Others have adapted too well to pain; they convince themselves that they can tough it out, rather than finding ways to actively challenge a painful reality. But not all pain is good pain!

Others simply see endings as wrong, and the reasons are complex. For some, an ending implies failure. For others, especially if endings require confrontation, their map tells them to avoid the pain. Then for others, where endings require hurting someone, their map tells them that causing pain to others is wrong. Cloud looks at each of these problems in relation to the internal maps we carry. Each of these internal maps prevents us from making an appropriate response to adaptive challenge. Let's review these unhelpful maps one by one.

The first map is denial. Some of us have learned a high pain threshold. Athletes commonly adapt to pain in this way, knowing that pain comes with the territory of high performance. As a result, we may fail to distinguish between good pain and bad pain because we have become adept at denying that pain exists. When we are leading an organization, those around us may be feeling the pain of missed expectations or waning effectiveness, while we are still smiling and feeling that life is rosy. The challenge is to begin listening more carefully to those around us, and observing signs of stress or grief or other kinds of pain.

The second map is codependence. This internal map prevents an adaptive response by telling us that we are responsible for the way others feel or perform. This is a common trait of oldest children who become caregivers for their younger siblings. People who grew up with responsibility for others often have the most difficult time confronting team members who consistently under-perform, or who may actually be functioning in a role for which they are not suited. A consequence is that an entire organization may suffer, or a team may struggle to make progress. I recall working with an elder who saw the writing on the wall, and was aware that the church had no more than six months of financial liquidity, yet could not face the sale of the building. As a result he guaranteed that the transition would be even more difficult, or might be completely out of control in a "crash and burn" scenario.

Others possess an internal map that tells them that an ending means a failure. On a warm spring day in Hamilton I met a stockbroker who had had a particularly bad year after several years of success. He related that after the loss of his father, he had trouble selling stocks that were not performing. He held on too long, and lost money he should not have lost. Somehow folding his cards, even when it was the right thing to do, had become an emotional load he couldn't handle. It had taken some months of counselling and working through his grief for him to get back on track. Most endings are not "bad" so much as necessary, and wisdom is knowing what is necessary pain and what is not. Commitment to a particular goal means embracing certain kinds of endings along the way.

The fourth is the map of loyalty. This particular kind of software might have been the experience of the elder I mentioned above. When this internal map is in conflict with a particular ending, people get stuck. I recall talking to a leader whose organization was in trouble, and who needed to make an adaptive response. The changes required meant new personnel, and the younger leader he had been mentoring for three years would suddenly find himself out of his depth. Actually, the younger man simply lacked the relational skillset required to navigate the coming changes.

The older leader had had a mixed relationship with his own father, who had failed to be there for him. He saw his mentoring relationship like that of a father, a very positive frame, but one that now conflicted with the need in his organization. Eventually he came to see that his failure to be honest about the road ahead would become a problem not just for the organization, but for the younger man he had mentored. Inevitably he would crash and burn. An honest conversation would offer a supportive road forward, and help the young man grow in understanding his own gifts and capacities.

Getting to Hopelessness

All four maps prevent an adaptive response, and ensure that a stuck organization will remain stuck. We may find ourselves in a liminal space, generated by forces outside our control, and without any ability to move forward.

What generates a particular adaptive response is unpredictable. Humans, like the organizations they create, are adept at denial. But we are also good at learning when the conditions are right. Wearing a T-shirt may be appropriate clothing for a northern Ontario summer, but beyond September as the days get colder it becomes a good learning experience that generates a quick response!

But sometimes it takes more than changing conditions to challenge our resistance to change. Sometimes reality has to sit up and smack us with a two-by-four. Remember Gonzales' description of the behaviours of lost people? The last two are these:

People realize they can no longer deny that they're lost. Fear and panic set in, and their brains stop working. Now every action they take is senseless, creating more fatigue and more problems.

Confused and panicked, people search frantically for any sign that's familiar. But they *are* lost, so this strategy fails and they continue to deteriorate.

The next step is surrender: recognizing we are out of our depth. In fact, the situation is hopeless, and hopelessness is sometimes exactly what we need.

Hopelessness can move a system to instability, like the emotional crisis of the physicists working with quantum reality. And nothing mobilizes us like this sense that there is no solution, that we are heading for a train wreck. The old proverb puts it well: "When the going gets tough, the tough get going."

We all need hope for the future, but sometimes hope becomes a magical wishing for change in the face of evidence to the contrary, a powerful force that can fuel denial. No matter the reality we face, we can hang on to some imaginary reality, some sense that it can't be this bad. The "hope" in hopelessness is that we are finally through denial and squarely facing reality. The experience can be mystical: a sense of abandonment to God, the moment of surrender. In Alcoholics Anonymous it's called Step One: "we are powerless" and "our lives are unmanageable." Hopelessness can lead to surrender, and surrender can be the trigger that allows us to fully embrace the new reality we find ourselves in. It can empower what otherwise seemed impossible: a creative and adaptive response.

Some organizations never make it to this point; abandoning the old way is just too costly. This is particularly the case when the need doesn't seem urgent. After all, we say to ourselves, the world is still buying green widgets. Maybe we can stretch it out for two more years. Meantime a new company is designing striped orange widgets, and by the time we begin thinking about adaptation someone else has already done the work.

Hitting "the wall"

> Sometimes the best map will not guide you,
> You can't see what's round the bend,
> Sometimes the road leads through dark places
> Sometimes the darkness is your friend. (Cockburn, 1995)

Most of us have had the experience of using an out-dated map. If your discovery of being lost occurred when you were already under pressure, say, pulling into an unfamiliar town at midnight, then it was all the more distressing. You literally don't know what is around the bend.

Yet, "sometimes the darkness is your friend." This line from a song by Bruce Cockburn highlights the complexity of life and growth. Transitions are rarely comfortable and are frequently complex, yet often they lead into wider, brighter spaces that would never have been found had we followed the well-trod paths.

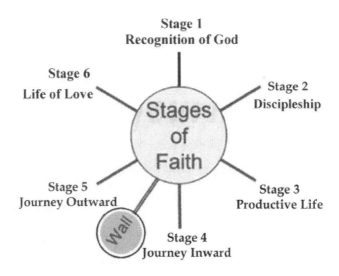

Figure 2. Stages of Faith

In *The Critical Journey* Janet Hagberg and Robert Guelich describe six stages on the journey of faith. Stages three to five are of particular interest, because they describe the movement from a productive life, to a place of confusion, and from there to a new place of restful action. Our present interest is in that transitional place between stages 4 and 5. They call it "the wall." (Hagberg & Guelich, 2005, p. 114-130).

Stage 3 is the "normal" productive life. It's busy. There are multiple and complex demands, with little time for reflection. Then something goes wrong and we are launched into liminal space. The most notable description of stage 4 is: "Things just aren't working anymore," and "There's got to be more." I don't know how many pastors and leaders I have spoken with in the past ten years who find themselves in this squeeze.

Sharon Parks describes the experience of "shipwreck" in the lives of young adults, those times when young adults experience something unexpected or disappointing. She writes, "These experiences often became the context in which big questions emerged in powerful ways." She explains that technology has made life transitions harder than they used to be. Digital devices and social networking "can contribute to heightened productivity and a greater connection to the global community; yet [also to an] increasing sense of loneliness and isolation that leads to many mental and physical health risks." (Parks, 2007).

But these conditions don't apply only to young adults; they apply to leaders in a variety of struggling organizations. New realities reflect a more brittle economy. There is more at stake in choices these days, and less certainty about where the path will lead. Big questions emerge, and the answers are not apparent. The pressure to make decisions increases along with the uncertainty of outcomes. The old map tells us to stay safe. Yet we desperately need leaders who will take risks, who will depend on God to lead us to an unknown future, and who know that quick fixes only push the tough decisions further down the track.

From Dis-Orientation to Orientation

Another way of framing the transition between stage 4 and 5 is the movement from a stable state of apparent orientation, through disorientation, to re-orientation. When our internal maps suddenly become inadequate, the experience is one of profound disorientation. Like Killip on the mountain, we are lost.

But these transition experiences are not new. Our heroes of faith were familiar with uncertainty and with disorientation. According to the

65

author of Hebrews Abraham went out, "not knowing..." (11:8). Walter Brueggemann sees the movement from orientation to disorientation in the prayers of the Psalmists and the Prophets. (Brueggemann, 2001).

First are prayers of orientation. The words of Psalm 1 present the kind of black and white world most of us live in before the great questions rise to disturb our clay. In this simple world the good guys are blessed and the bad guys get what's coming to them. This is the world before 9/11 and Aleppo. Then comes the crash, and suddenly we find more affinity with Jeremiah in Lamentations 3:1: "I am the one who has seen affliction." *Where are you God?* Our questions echo a sense of abandonment when a predictable world has become unstable. We no longer know who God is. God has become like a predator: like a vicious bear lying in wait for his victim (Lam 3-5).

Our experience of sovereign presence has become something other, like *sovereign absence*. If we make it through this phase, eventually we come out the far end with a different perspective. We are re-oriented to God and God's world.

> But this I call to mind,
> and therefore I have hope:
> The steadfast love of the Lord never ceases,
> His mercies never come to an end.
> They are new every morning;
> Great is your faithfulness!   (Lam 3:21-24)

If we pass through the uncertainty, we can discover new purpose. Sharon Parks writes, "If we do survive shipwreck – if we wash up on a new shore, perceiving more adequately how life really is – there is gladness. It is gladness that pervades one's whole being; there is a new sense of vitality, be it quiet or exuberant. Usually, however, there is more than relief in this gladness. There is transformation. We discover a new reality behind the loss . . ." (Parks, 1999, p. 29)

"Shipwreck" experiences are a part of the much larger journey of developing a deeper sense of meaning and purpose. They can result in a richer, more personal faith and become the foundation of new exploration. In organizations, they result in renewed engagement and energy and open up new territory, or in what is termed a competitive advantage. Our personal sense of control was inadequate and unrealistic. We have surrendered to something larger than ourselves.

In classical spirituality, we call this experience of hitting the wall the dark night of the soul. The hope of the Dark Night is that we are like the caterpillar who weaves a cocoon and emerges transformed.

In the experience of the Dark Night, God seems distant and silent. But the silence is fraught with purpose. In this experience of abandonment, our soul is purged of self-motivations. The experience is one of soul-searching and of purification, the kind of desperate reflection we avoid when things are going well. And so God engineers a way for us to slow down, perhaps even to stop. The pain gets our attention in a way that daily victory and constant activity do not.

In the Old Testament narrative Israel is led by God into the desert because only in this way can she learn radical dependence on God. Daily she is fed by God, given water by God, and delivered from her enemies by God. By day she is led by the cloud, and by night by the pillar of fire. God leads Israel into the desert to woo her. Exodus is a great romance. The Lord will allow no other lovers for Israel.

This is the great value of the desert; it purges us of distorted motives and wrong attachments. In the desert we detach from things and from self in order to become attached to God and his kingdom. Only after forty years in the desert is Israel ready to enter the land of promise. But what are the mechanisms God employs for this purpose? St. John and St. Gregory describe the process in terms of the wounding of the soul, of *compunction*.

The word was originally a medical term, and described acute attacks of pain. Translated into the spiritual life, it describes a pain in the soul, a pain that arises from two causes: the existence of sin, and our hunger for God. Compunction is an act of the Spirit in us, an act by which God awakens us. But this awakening is painful, like the thawing of a frozen limb, or the renewed use of a limb which was neglected. We are pierced by love, and the attention of the soul is recalled to God. (Leclercq, 1982, p. 30). St. John of the Cross describes the process in his *Spiritual Canticle*:

> How manage breath on breath
> So long, my soul, not living where life is?
> Brought low and close to death
> by those arrows of his?
> Love was the bow. I know. I've witnesses.
> And wounds to show. You'd cleave
> clean to the heart, and never think of healing?
> Steal it, and when you leave
> leave it? What sort of dealing,
> to steal and never keep, and yet keep stealing? (Juan & Nims, 1979, p. 5)

The most prominent characteristic of the poems of compunction are paradox. We attempt to describe spiritual truth in human language, and end up with contradictions. "Steal and keep stealing; wounds of love . . ." these categories are paradoxical, but not unfamiliar in our experience. Any lover knows the wounding of the soul, a desire that seems insatiable, the experience of awakening as if from sleep when suddenly all the world seems new. Suddenly the ego is suppressed and we think of nothing but the good of the one we love. Our own needs seem unimportant. The beloved is all in all. What but love can wean us away from the enticement of this world? This was the essence of the monastic testimony, that "God is not known if not loved." Bernard of Clairvaux writes, "Your blessings and love are like hands and feet to help me gently move toward You and Your absolute and sovereign love. But such an experience is not to be enjoyed with unmitigated pleasure. Instead, it is one of yearnings, struggles, and frustrations, mixed with bitter sweetness . . ." And:

So when my eyes of introspection get confused, dim, and even blind, I pray that You will open them quickly; not in shame as Adam's eyes were opened. Rather, may they be opened to behold Your glory (Exodus 33:18). Then, forgetting all about my own poverty and insignificance, my whole being may be able to stand up, to run into Your embrace of love, and see You whom I love, and love You whom I have yet to see . . . (Clairvaux & Tompkins, 1983, p. 112)

The Dark Night is a gift to us: a gift intended to bring wakefulness and humility. When leaders and faith communities are in decline, they begin to ask new questions, deep questions, about motivation, about ends and means, and about control. The Lord engineers the journey so that our eyes are lifted above our own needs and the small kingdoms we build to the eternal kingdom he alone can build.

The disorientation arrives for the purpose of renewal. God puts to death what is earthly in us so that his life can fill us instead, and so that eventually we can renew our ministry and mission with our sole aim of pleasing our Master. We feel caught. The call is to enter a holding space – a place between. There is no going back and no going forward.

But neither is it empty space: it is God space, sacred space. In the paradoxical reality of spiritual life, at the still point we discover the dance. We can freely embrace God's gift of liminality. We aren't lost; *we are right here.*

Can we learn to navigate between two worlds? Can we learn to dwell in the space where we are not in control and we don't know the answers? Can we answer God's call to be where we are?

When my children were young, they enjoyed all kinds of games. But we played one game I never really understood. When I was lounging around, they loved to come and sit on my lap. Sometimes as a kind of hug, I would put my arms around them and grip their ankles and hold them in a vice grip. They would squeal and struggle. But so long as they were small enough to sit on my lap, I was strong enough that they could not break free. They loved this game! Now much later in life, I realize that there was a security in their inability to move. They learned a kind of surrender to the strength of a father. When we are ready, the Lord will teach us that kind of stillness. Then when we are ready again, he'll let go.

At the still point of the turning world. Neither flesh nor fleshless;
Neither from nor towards; at the still point, there the dance is,
But neither arrest nor movement. And do not call it fixity,
Where past and future are gathered.
Neither movement from nor towards,
Neither ascent nor decline. Except for the point, the still point,
There would be no dance, and there is only the dance.

TS Eliot, Four Quartets. "Burnt Norton, II"

CHAPTER 3

Holding Space

Iceland's Silfra fissure, in Thingvellir National Park, is a gap between continents formed by the constant pulling apart of two tectonic plates. It fills with some of the clearest water in the world, the result of a natural filtration process where melting waters from the nearby Langjökull glacier pass through porous underground lava for thirty to 100 years before arriving in the fissure. The chance to swim between tectonic plates is irresistible for those who are looking for a new experience, and a number of tourist experiences are marketed for swimmers.

The movement of tectonic plates shapes continents and mountain ranges, and creates the most defining features of earth's geography. Gradual movement of plates define our world; sudden movements can destroy civilizations. But tectonic shifts can be other than physical, and the effects equally dramatic.

Today we are swimming between two colliding worlds, and the pressure is enormous. It's tense: we realize that everything around us might fall. We fear the unpredictability of the forces. Our illusions of control collapse. We share the anxiety of those around us, and as familiar structures disintegrate we wonder what will take their place.

While the demands on our own emotional and spiritual resources increase, we find ourselves working harder and for less gain. We are caught in the law of decreasing returns.

Sometimes the wisest action we can take is to find a way to withdraw and to rest. In the West we equate stillness with inactivity and escape. In biblical and Eastern thought it's different: emptiness and stillness are not equated with inactivity, but with renewal. We "cease striving" so that we can discover God (Ps 46:10). We admit that our own power and perspective are limited and finite. In our weakness, God is our strength (Ps 46:1). In order to save our lives, we must lose them.

Nature supplies us with other examples of wisdom. The book of Proverbs reveals the author's fondness for insects. Consider the butterfly. It starts out in the world as a rather ugly caterpillar. When the caterpillar spins a cocoon its life moves inward: its whole world collapses to a tiny point. It closes the life it knew and withdraws from the world completely. It endures this season for as long as biological necessity has determined; then suddenly the cocoon opens and a new life emerges. The world is engaged from a fresh perspective. If that stillness and inwardness had not occurred, there would have been no new beginning and no fresh possibilities. *We are not what we were, and not yet what we will become.*

For the caterpillar the place of fixity is a pregnant pause. Transformation occurs in the hiddenness of the cocoon. It is a paradox. What appears as inaction is in fact a marshalling of new strength and resources. Just as Jesus emptied himself in order to serve God's purpose, so we too embrace the call to empty ourselves for the sake of the kingdom. This call doesn't come only to individuals. Entire organizations and communities must sometimes choose descent in order to discover new potential.

The following diagram, adapted from *Presence*, illustrates a pattern of organizational renewal. On the left side we move down the curve; on the right side we re-engage and discover a new future.

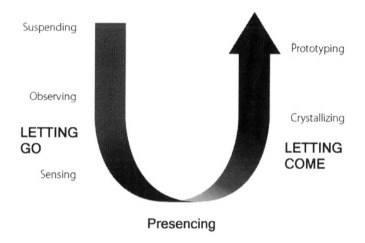

Descent and Ascent

Peter Senge and his coworkers describe a pattern of organizational renewal that reflects the insights of complexity and adaptive science. They describe the paradoxical nature of descent and emptiness, the importance of surrender to something larger than ourselves. Moving down the left side of the U describes the process of letting go until at the bottom, in the space between letting go and letting come, something miraculous can happen. No ascent, no decline, and no movement - yet also no fixity. At the still point, and in the clarity of the space between, things occur which we can really only accept as a gift.

Otto Scharmer tells the story of a loss that occurred when he was sixteen years old. (Senge, Scharmer, Jaworski, & Flowers, 2005, p. 79-81) Otto was at school, and halfway through the day the principal called him out of class and sent him home: she didn't say why. He walked as quickly as he could to the train station and attempted to call home, but got no answer. After the forty-five-minute train ride he took a cab rather than the usual bus.

Long before he arrived he saw a huge gray-black cloud of smoke rising in the air. The long, tree-lined driveway that led to the farm was choked with hundreds of neighbours, firefighters and police. He jumped from the cab and ran the last half mile.

When he reached the courtyard he couldn't believe the sight. The huge 350-year-old farmhouse where his family had lived for generations was gone. There was nothing left but a smouldering ruin. He felt as if someone had removed the ground from under his feet. The place of his birth, childhood and youth was lost to him forever.

As his gaze sank deeper into the flames, the flames seemed to enter his own being. He felt time slowing down. In that moment he realized how deep his attachment had been to the house, and to his familiar world. But then he became aware of what was left: a tiny element of his essential self was unaltered. He, the seer, was still here, and the whole dimension of his self was intact. He suddenly knew that his true self was alive, awake and more acutely present than ever before. At that critical moment, with everything gone, he felt released and free to encounter that part of his deep self that would persist into a new future.

The next day his grandfather arrived. He was 87 years old and had worked all his life on the farm. Summoning all the energy he had, he got out of the car and walked straight to where Otto's father was working on the cleanup. He didn't even turn his head toward the smoking ruins of the place where he had spent his entire life. He took his son's hand and said simply, "Keep your head up, my boy. Look forward." (Senge, Scharmer, Jaworski, & Flowers, 2005, p. 81). Otto's grandfather focused all his energy on shifting the attention from the past, to the future.

Losing one's ancestral home at sixteen is a profound loss, and would be a setback to any family. Winston Churchill once described leadership as going from failure to failure without losing enthusiasm.

Failure and success are complex categories, and meaningless apart from a context. In business fitness is used to describe the competitive edge. In the world of biology, researchers use the term to describe the success of an organism. Higher degrees of fitness are depicted by linear height on a landscape, and a loss of fitness is visualized as going downhill. When a species is threatened, as happened with the coyote in America, it descends the fitness landscape to the edge of chaos.

Fitness depends on numerous interrelated factors that can combine in endless variety. There are three types of fitness landscapes, and each can be used to characterize familiar scenarios:

1. gradual, like the undulating terrain of southern California. This environment no longer exists in the world of business and isn't likely to return.

2. rugged, like the topography of Nepal – comparable to the today's competition in the cellular industry.

3. random, like the topography of the moon, where the impact of meteors rather than the logic of plate tectonics shaped the surface.

The coyote had to cope with habitat destruction, encroachment by human population, and even outright attempts to eradicate it. If a species adapts, it may result in increased fitness that is even better than the original habitat. In the case of the coyote and the foothills around Malibu, California, this is what occurred.

The struggle to secure a niche is described as an uphill climb. But when a species reaches a subsidiary peak (called a local optimum) on the fitness landscape, it may choose to remain there. Biologists call this perch a *basin of attraction* – a rest stop during the competitive journey. But species become stranded on these peaks. (Pascale, Milleman, Gioja, 2000, p. 103). They work hard to get there, and are reluctant to leave. But because there are no bridges to get to the higher peaks, the organism must go down to go up.

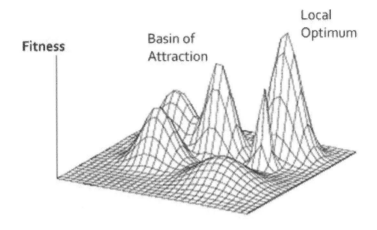

Figure 4. Fitness Landscape

In order to make this shift, there has to be sufficient instability or challenge; otherwise, an organism will not opt to leave the intermediate peak and suffer the unknown prospects of the valley. Abandon a ministry while it is still successful? *Never!* Leave a comfortable job, however dull, with all its benefits? *Why?*

Living systems are driven out of a basin of attraction by discomfort – whether internal or external. Employee unrest, new competition, dwindling food sources, customer defection, loss of margins: all these can combine to generate unrest.

Fitness landscapes are useful tools in navigating the edge of chaos. They have two important advantages over more traditional journey maps. First, the landscape imagery makes clear that one must "go down to go up" if the goal is to reach a higher fitness peak. The human disruption and distress associated with this movement are often the undermanaged aspect of corporate change. Second, like walking on a trampoline, the landscape changes as soon as there is movement on it.

The living systems view does not focus only on the path of an organism as it maneuvers across the competitive landscape. Complexity also concerns itself with the way *the landscape itself* changes as the organism moves across it. Systems dynamics sees the challenge as mapping causal factors that move a system from point A to point B. Complexity regards the journey as walking on a trampoline. Each step alters the whole topography. What was "up" at the start may be somewhat "down" farther along the route, and the ascent may be far steeper as the destination draws near. (Pascale, Milleman, Gioja, 2000, p. 106)

North American evangelical churches arrived at a fitness peak in the 1970s and 80s. In a stable and settled culture, the Christian story was accepted and even had a certain dominance. But our impact on the culture around us was waning. Growth by conversion was on the decline, even though some smaller and marginal groups were having success. Church Growth gurus were advocating the seeker model and the homogenous growth model. Some growth resulted, but it was mono-cultural, a kind of growth that is particularly susceptible to disease. Much of the seeker sensitive movement pandered to the appetites of religious consumers. The tourist approach to life was not one that fostered depth or commitment.

The pace of change accelerated. Modernity was passing away and we were confronted with a new reality. But few groups were prepared to do the work of descending into the valley to relearn how to engage with the culture. Many of those that made the effort were too accommodating. The voices calling for renewal were too threatening and so we continued to marginalize the innovators and missional leaders, who joined parachurch groups where they could express missional passion and vision. This further accelerated our decline. We circled the wagons and did business as usual. Meanwhile, the cultural shift accelerated, leaving us even more isolated and increasingly fearful of changes that we did not understand.

In some places, serious efforts were made to go through the pain needed to reengage. Some leaders and churches descended from their peaks or "basins of attraction." This was often precipitated by desperation, and sometimes brought renewal and birthed new initiatives. In the UK and Australia there was FORGE and Fresh Expressions. The Gospel and our Culture Network formed in Canada and the US and produced the volume *Missional Church* and the follow-up, *Treasure in Jars of Clay* and hundreds of thoughtful articles. Practitioners and academics, front-line workers and pastors were asking new questions in the face of decline. Books like *The Younger Evangelicals* (2002) developed taxonomies for the shifting movements at the close of Christendom. In a time of apparent collapse, an era of renewed theological creativity was opening. But it wasn't enough.

How the Future Finds Us

Stand still. The trees ahead and bushes beside you
Are not lost. Wherever you are is called Here,
And you must treat it as a powerful stranger,
Must ask permission to know it and be known.
The forest breathes. Listen. It answers,
I have made this place around you.
If you leave it, you may come back again, saying Here.
No two trees are the same to Raven.
No two branches are the same to Wren.
If what a tree or a bush does is lost on you,
You are surely lost. Stand still. The forest knows
Where you are. You must let it find you. – David Wagoner
(Whyte, 2002)

The sense of lostness is always contextual. To the degree we understand and see our context, we are not lost. And if we are quiet enough, still enough, we may hear whispers of the future.

The knee-jerk reaction is analysis. The trouble with analysis is that it is not whole-sighted; it's almost purely left-brained and mono-dimensional. As the tension increases most of us get caught in the snare, caught in the words, instead of moving toward the reality the words seek to instill. We confuse the menu for the meal. We are too busy to listen, driven by the expectations of those around us, and by leadership models left over from the age of expansion. Harried and anxious, we invest more and more of our limited fund of energy in efforts at maintaining control, efforts that we already know will not pay us back. But others expect us to "take leadership," to lead boldly and forge ahead, even when we intuitively know the need is for stillness and reflection.

What makes the challenge so intense is that not only do we base our actions on the conditions of yesterday, we base our *seeing* on the mental models we built from our experience of the past. Biologists Humberto Maturana and Francisco Varela report that more than eighty percent of the visual information we use to create visual perceptions of the world comes from information already inside the brain. "Information from outside only slightly perturbs a system; it never functions as objective instructions." (Wheatley, 2005, p. 37).

When we use old maps to attempt to find our way forward in new conditions, we see what we are prepared to see, with our mental models reflecting past experience. Like Ken Killip on the mountainside, our mind is already guided by a mental model. This is why we note that a living system cannot be directed, it can only be disturbed. How do we get to the place where we suspend our models and see afresh in a new location? Henri Nouwen relates an old story from Chuang Tzu: "The purpose of a fish trap is to catch fish and when the fish are caught, the trap is forgotten. The purpose of a rabbit snare is to catch rabbits.

When the rabbits are caught, the snare is forgotten. The purpose of the word is to convey ideas. When the ideas are grasped, the words are forgotten. Where can I find a man who has forgotten words? He is the one I would like to talk to." (Nouwen, 1981, p. 49)

Paradox marks the way forward; knowledge itself is the problem.[2] When we confuse information with knowledge, even our maps will fail us. The need is to build new maps from a place of inner quiet, free from the pressure of action and decision-making. We need to draw on ancient disciplines of contemplation and trust. The hope is to attain an inner knowing that accesses a reality that has not yet emerged. This is a different *kind* of knowing.

When Otto stood in front of his burning home and his gaze went from the fire to a place of inner knowledge, the shift was already occurring. He moved from seeing the immediate details to accessing his inner self. In that quiet place of presence he discovered inner freedom. This sort of knowledge is an inner knowing, an invitation to move beyond ourselves toward our life's purpose. The task is really to become superb listeners. Heidegger wrote that waiting, listening, was the most profound way to serve God.

> My life is not this steeply sloping hour
> in which you see me hurrying.
> Much stands behind me; I stand before it like a tree;
> I am only one of my many mouths,
> and at that, the one that will be still the soonest.
> I am the rest between two notes,
> which are somehow always in discord
> because Death's note wants to climb over --

---

[2] "All men and women exist in a state of epistemological pilgrimage." Paul Helm, *Faith and Understanding* (Eerdmans, 1997)

but in the dark interval, reconciled,
they stay there trembling,
And the song goes on, beautiful. (Rilke & Bly, 1981)

A song is not a single note. Concentrating on the notes themselves, we lose the beauty of the whole, the relationship of each note to the next, and equally importantly, the space between the notes. Inspiration often depends on our ability to let go of the need for control, even for control of our perceptions, and to simply be present and open.

Some time ago a friend related to me that the physicists who are researching quantum dynamics and working with the very smallest particles came up against another mystery. While there were some things that were definable, one of the largest questions remaining was about the power in matter. No one knows where it comes from. This caused one scientist to theorize that perhaps the power is in the blank spaces.

Blank spaces are what we lose when we organize. Blank spaces are those elements of shared life that remain shrouded in mystery. In fact, community itself is a mystery. You can plan it, organize it, pray for it and still not get it. It requires something spontaneous and unreachable by human effort and thought alone. It requires an ability to see the implicit wholeness of the collective. It requires more weakness than strength, and we aren't very good at weakness. Community is a gift, and we aren't good at receiving it. Eugene Peterson writes,

The secularized mind is terrorized by mysteries. Thus it makes lists, labels people, assigns roles, and solves problems. But a solved life is a reduced life. These tightly buttoned-up people never take great faith risks or make convincing love talk. They deny or ignore the mysteries and diminish human existence to what can be managed, controlled, and fixed. We live in a cult of experts who explain and solve. The vast technological apparatus around us gives the impression that there is a tool for everything if we can only afford it. (Peterson, 1989, p. 65)

So we listen and we wait. We wait without knowing, for knowing
would be knowledge of the wrong thing. We wait without
certainty, for certainty would be trust in the wrong thing.
Who waits for what he has not heard? And who listens for what
he does not know? The true listener moves beyond the noise of
expectation and desire to wait in stillness for the Word.
There is yet faith
But the faith and the love and the hope are all in the waiting.
T.S. Eliot, "Little Gidding, V"

Three Conditions for Emergence

When social and cultural plates are colliding, the shaking
generates tremendous change, and change in turn generates
tremendous anxiety. The challenge is to pray the prayer of indifference.
One of the outcomes for a non-anxious presence is a new set of
questions. As Sharon Parks pointed out, the big questions that rise to
the surface become powerful motivators – they constitute strange
attractors – around which new life can organize itself. Margaret
Wheatley describes three conditions for self-organizing systems:
identity, information, and relationship. Identity is the sense-making
capacity of the organization, and information is its medium.
Relationships are the pathways to the intelligence of the system
(Wheatley, 1996).

All organizations begin with an intention, a belief that is founded
in the larger power of the whole. People come together for a purpose, a
belief that something is possible now that the group is together. Once
this identity coheres, it becomes the sense-making process of the
organization. A system refers back to its sense of self in order to make
decisions and to interpret data and events.

But as noted above, systems use information they already possess
to make sense of something new. Identity includes history and hopes,
memories and dreams. A healthy system gives weight to both its past

and its future. The clearer the organizations identity, the more readily they can incorporate new data and navigate a chaotic and fluid environment. Where identity has devolved to roles and functions, this becomes more difficult. The system must be disturbed.

Information is at the heart of life. Information is like DNA – it informs structure and purpose, and enables adaptive responses. When a system assigns meaning to data, it "in-forms" it. Data becomes information when it is interpreted and absorbed.

Living systems thrive on the edge between stability and chaos. In this region new information can enter, but the organization retains its identity. Pushing against equilibrium, systems seek this dynamic region in order to stay alive. If a system is too strongly ordered, it begins to die. If it lives too much with chaos, it loses its memory. A fixation on internal order creates resistance to new information. A fixation on change creates anxiety and chaos, and information overload.

When information flows freely to everyone in the organization, the eyes and ears of an organization are multiplied. Its sensory abilities increase, and thus its ability to discover subtle changes in the environment, enabling an adaptive response. The wider the network, the greater the flow of information. TS Eliot asks,

Where is the Life we have lost in living?
Where is the wisdom we have lost in knowledge?
Where is the knowledge we have lost in information? (Eliot, 1990)

Relationships are the pathway to the intelligence of the system. Information is created and transformed in relationships. Likewise the organization's identity is created and clarified as people have access to one another, and this opens new possibilities. Without these connections, nothing happens. Relationships are the living organizational chart. To respond to adaptive challenges in a timely manner, people need access to the intelligence of the whole system. The wider the network, the greater the knowledge.

Where connections are strong, the system expands to include more and more of the members as stakeholders. Trust is rooted and grows where connection is fostered, and this enables greater risks in relationships as well as in adaptive responses. The more the organization knows itself, the more discerning it becomes, enabling investment in new relationships and new challenges.

When Dave Harder arrived in Ottawa in 2000 he arrived as pastor of an aging Mennonite congregation in the urban core. Many other churches had already abandoned the core, which their members had earlier fled, choosing the safer and cleaner suburbs. This old church was stubborn, however. Its members had felt called to the urban environment, and many of them still resided there. But they were greying; they were losing touch with the urban context, which had changed drastically over the years. They didn't know if they had the energy needed to reengage. But they were willing to try, and they were willing to change.

They leveraged existing relationships to connect with newcomers. They discovered many new immigrant families who were already people of faith, and others who were open to friendship and hospitality. Some, who had retired from government jobs and who knew the ropes in the civil service, became advocates for the immigrant families who had difficulty navigating bureaucracy and accessing services. Word spreads. They spun off a new ministry as a non-profit. They planted a second church meeting in a storefront. Suddenly they were connecting with street people, many who would not enter a church but who welcomed a coffee and conversation. It was messy. Funds were always tight. New members had little to give financially, but were willing to give time. A young moms' ministry was born, led by a recent immigrant from Somalia who had a degree in social work.

Suddenly their reach expanded again, and they were connecting with young families living in poverty and minimum-wage jobs. They connected with a group of advocates pushing for fair wages, and began a justice ministry that leveraged the efforts of two mainline churches nearby. They spun off a daughter church because the storefront was too crowded on Sunday mornings. Now fifteen years along, the Journey Network is six churches strong, but their social impact belies their small size.

Paradox and Ascent

Slow down, you've moving too fast

You got to make the morning last– (Simon & Garfunkel, 1966)

In the past several years two of my friends have walked the Camino de Santiago across France and Spain. This ancient route, nearly 800 kilometres in length, has been traveled by pilgrims for over a thousand years.

It's a grueling trek. Even with modern shoes and equipment, it isn't for the faint-hearted. Yet the Camino continues to draw walkers of all types: some lean and in good shape, others who would rarely leave their desks except for a cup of coffee. Most have only a partial idea what they are up against. The inner journey turns out to be just as demanding as the outward one.

Those who walk the Camino say that the spiritual and emotional and physical journeys merge on the long days of walking. What begins as a walk morphs into pilgrimage, a liminal space, an encounter with the deep self. Though most walk with others, and though there is plenty of time for interaction with other pilgrims along the way, it's the face in the mirror that becomes the real encounter. Through the fatigue, the bad weather, the blistered feet, the hunger, the heavy pack, the lack of distraction – there is no place for pretence, no place to hide. Even some of those who begin as tourists end as pilgrims. Parker Palmer writes,

Treacherous terrain, bad weather, taking a fall, getting lost -- challenges of that sort, largely beyond our control, can strip the ego of the illusion that it is in charge and make space for true self to emerge. If that happens, the pilgrim has a better chance to find the sacred center he or she seeks. Disabused of our illusions by much travel and travail, we awaken one day to find that the sacred center is here and now -- in every moment of the journey, everywhere in the world around us, and deep within our own hearts. (Palmer, 2000, p. 18)

Leaders who survive grueling conditions are those who have moved from sleeping to wakefulness. Maybe it's the pain of the blisters that calls them out. Maybe it's a bad leadership experience or a broken marriage. But something has happened that is like a cold wave dashed against the face. Something like teetering at the edge of an icy cliff and looking down on the rocks below. Plastic piety gives way to real questions. Mariners like to say there are no atheists on a stormy sea.

When our outward journey becomes an inward journey the first thing we discover is paradox. The second is humility. Curiously, these are also the first things addicts discover as they move into recovery. It's not willpower that gets us into recovery, but something more like a gift. Yet it's still I who must choose. *I choose…* yet I admit I am powerless. We were addicted to success and its rewards, to busyness and its sense of urgency. We were climbing the ladder; *that's what normal people do, right?*

Paradox. The ability to hold in tension things that look like opposites. Night and day; hot and cold; ascent and descent; success and failure; up and down; faith and doubt. But the ability to live in the space between allows us to negotiate with reality, to *form a relationship with the unknown*. We move beyond binaries to integration. We move beyond the narrow focus of the problem to see the larger context.

Harlan Cleveland writes that "the art of . . . leadership is above all the leader's capacity to hold contradictory propositions comfortably in a mind that relishes complexity." (Cleveland, 2002, p. 197). Yet surely opposites are opposites? Perhaps, yet the relationship between binaries like success and failure are easily seen in the lives of great leaders.

Winston Churchill was nearly sixty years old when he lost his seat in Parliament. He spent his days painting and penning articles for a variety of journals. He struggled to pay the bills. It seemed he would never feel truly useful again. Then an unlikely combination of events propelled him back into the public sphere. His peculiar blend of wit, courage, and doggedness enabled him to lead his nation – against all odds – and win, against the most heinous threat to civilization in the last century. Perhaps it was their finest hour.

We too may find ourselves with a degree of success, but the writing is on the wall. We can no longer move forward and any other choice looks like failure. There are no bridges to get us to the higher peaks, and no supplemental oxygen either. We must "go down to go up." It requires immense inner resolve; and sometimes, of course, the choice is not ours!

Through the centuries the theological motifs of ascent and descent have battled for dominance. Henry Wadsworth Longfellow in his poem, *The Ladder of St. Augustine*, captures well the metaphor of ascent.

> We have not wings, we cannot soar;
>   But we have feet to scale and climb
> By slow degrees, by more and more,
>   The cloudy summits of our time.
> The mighty pyramids of stone
>   That wedge-like cleave the desert airs,
> When nearer seen, and better known,
>   Are but gigantic flights of stairs.
> The distant mountains, that uproar
>   Their solid bastions to the skies,
> Are crossed by pathways, that appear
>   As we to higher levels rise. (Longfellow, 2012)

Early in the twentieth century the Spanish philosopher Miguel de Unamuno told the European world that they had distorted the meaning of faith by aligning it with the Western philosophy of "progress" rather than what he saw in Scripture. Life is never a straight line forward, and nature seems as comfortable with disorder as with order. The West is enamored with images of success and its trappings: from air-brushed women to shiny, fast cars. Success is fine; but when a culture can *only* value ascent, it has some relearning to do. Life cannot be lived in a single dimension. And what do we do with a god who is vulnerable, and who surrenders power for weakness? As Peter Mayer asks in his song, *Fall* –

> What if the highest destination
> Of any given human life
> Was not a place that you could reach if
> You had to climb
> Wasn't up above like heaven
> So no need to fly at all
> What if to reach the highest place
> You had to fall? (Mayer, 2001)

H. Paul Santmire argues that the metaphor of ascent became *the* "spiritual motif" in Western theology. The other two metaphors were that of fecundity and the journey, and these two tend to cluster. When they do they become what he calls the "ecological motif." (Santmire, 1985, p. 16). The ecological motif is complex, because the metaphor of fecundity is rooted, like that of ascent, in the image of the overwhelming mountain. The difference is determined by vision and intention. One may climb the mountain with eyes fixed on heaven, or one may climb to gain a renewed perspective of the earth. In other words, one climber seeks escape, or exaltation, while the other seeks engagement. In the life of Jesus these motifs blend together. The Word becomes flesh, descends into our world to live, suffer, and die, and then he is raised up – not to remain in a distant heaven but *so that* he can fill all things (Eph. 4:10). The explicit call of the Cross is the downward journey, the journey in emptiness. We lose our lives so that we can find them.

When Nathan Rieger arrived at the Winnipeg Centre Vineyard in 1999 he was assuming leadership of a church plant that was just five years old. Moreover, the location of the meeting place was non-intuitive. The congregation was anchored in the poorest, most dangerous part of the city, where drug deals were the norm, sex was cheap, and gangs competed for turf.

In spite of the challenging conditions, the Vineyard had a purpose: to make a difference in this high-crime, high-casualty part of town. They had even managed to save enough for a down-payment on an old building. The trouble was, they were intimately connected with church planting efforts in Nepal, where crime wasn't a problem, but funds were scarce. Their down-payment would go a lot further toward a new building there, so they gave it away.

Meanwhile, they became aware of an old office building on Main Street, and they approached the owner, a Christian businessman, to see if they could use the main floor as a meeting place. They were willing to do the sweat equity to make it usable. He gave them the space for less than it was worth.

The building worked great for the Vineyard and for the street community around them, and they were growing and having an impact. The owner of the building approached them to see if they could also make use of the top two floors. It offered some office space as well as potential residential space. The Winnipeg Vineyard was excited and leveraged internal skills to do renovation work. Before they finished the project, and seeing God at work, the owner of the building decided to gift the entire property to them.

There is nothing predictable or even "normal" about this order of events. It's a story of faith, and of God's provision for a work he wanted done. In a risk-averse culture, Christians tell stories like that of Abram, who went out hearing God's call, believing in a city he had not seen. As a result of his faith and obedience, his willingness to risk a journey into the unknown, Abram received a new name and a legacy: Abraham, the father of nations. (Gen. 17.5)

It's not the safe, Western way of doing things. Working from our Enlightenment heritage, we like to have all our ducks in a row before we move into new territory. We want to survey the land, marshal the opinions of the experts, and minimize every risk factor. The problem is that scientific approach doesn't work so well when we are facing an adaptive challenge. A turbulent environment is not knowable. We can't anticipate the next wave or changes in the current. Our destination is a place where no one has been before.

The greatest and most fundamental problems of life are fundamentally unsolvable. They can never be solved, but only outgrown.

C.G. Jung

In order to arrive at what you do not know
You must go by a way which is the way of ignorance.
In order to possess what you do not possess
You must go by the way of dispossession.
In order to arrive at what you are not
You must go through the way in which you are not.
And what you do not know is the only thing you know
And what you own is what you do not own
And where you are is where you are not.

T.S. Eliot, "East Coker III"

Interlude

Liminal space is space between, a nowhere land where entire church communities now find themselves. It's a frightening place where we feel we are lost, wandering without a map. But it's also a place that is pregnant with possibility. Just as the horizon is not a horizon without the space between where we stand and the land far off, so our ability to occupy the space between grants meaning to the place we stand. Eventually it is that space that anchors our ability to launch out to new lands.

When old guides fail us, how do we locate ourselves? Mental maps provide orientation, but they also create limits. Something inside us must move into an open space where we can discover new information.

Today we are swimming between shifting tectonic plates. We experience the shaking and we share the anxiety of those around us. Rather than manage the crisis, sometimes the wisest action is to find a way to withdraw and to rest. In the West we equate stillness with inactivity. In biblical thought emptiness and stillness are open space. We "cease striving" so that we can discover God.

> There is an age when one teaches what one knows.
> But there follows another when one teaches
> what one does not know . . .

95

It comes, maybe now, the age of another experience:
that of unlearning...
Roland Barthes (Alves, 1990)

In *Presence,* Peter Senge and his coworkers describe a pattern of organizational renewal that reflects the insights of complexity and adaptive science. They describe the paradoxical nature of descent and emptiness, the importance of surrender to something larger than ourselves. Moving downward is not failure, but rather opens the process of letting go until at the bottom, in the space between letting go and letting come, something miraculous can happen. Neither movement from nor movement toward, yet also neither fixity.

For the caterpillar the place of fixity is a pregnant pause, a paradox. Transformation occurs in the hiddenness of the cocoon. What appears outwardly as inaction is in fact an inward marshalling of new strength and resources. Just as Jesus emptied himself in order to serve God's purpose, we embrace the call to empty ourselves for the sake of the kingdom. This call doesn't come only to individuals. Entire organizations and communities must sometimes choose descent in order to discover new potential.

At the still point, and in the clarity of the space between, things occur which we can really only accept as a gift.

If we dream alone, it remains merely a dream.
If many dream together,
then it is the beginning of a new reality . . . Elisabeth Fiorenza
(Neave, 1996)

How do we make a start when we lack knowledge? Many believe that we must know how to do something before we do it. If this were literally true, many of the great innovations would never have occurred. An alternative view is that the creative process is a dynamic learning process, and the best we can possibly have at the outset is a vision of where we want to be, and a hypothesis about how to get there. Then we "create and adjust." We learn how to do something truly new by doing it. Or as Native Americans have said, "We make the path by walking."

There is a difference between knowing the path,
And walking the path.

Jesus said that the only sign he would give is the sign of Jonah. Then he spent three days in the tomb. The Apostles Creed has another way of saying this: "he descended into hell." I'm not sure that I know what that means, but I think the authors of the Creed were profoundly wise to include the statement as a way of saying once and for all that to be like the Master in all things, we would have to learn the promise of descent.

> When we win it's with small things,
> and the triumph itself makes us small.
> What is extraordinary and eternal
> does not want to be bent by us.
> I mean the Angel who appeared
> to the wrestlers of the Old Testament:
> when the wrestler's sinews
> grew long like metal strings,
> he felt them under his fingers
> like chords of deep music.
> Whoever was beaten by this Angel
> (who often simply declined the fight)
> went away proud and strengthened
> and great from that harsh hand,
> that kneaded him as if to change his shape.
> Winning does not tempt that man.
> This is how he grows: by being defeated, decisively,
> by constantly greater beings.
> Rainer Maria Rilke (Rilke, 1981)

In U-Theory, the only way up is the way down. At the bottom of the U, individuals or groups on the journey come to a threshold that requires a "letting go" of everything that is not essential. This threshold recalls the words of Jesus that. "It is easier for a camel to go through the eye of a needle than for a rich man to enter the kingdom of God" (Matt. 19.24). While we are riding the wave of success or popularity we become full of ourselves, and closed to other streams of information. The last thing we are thinking about is that the seed needs to fall into the ground and die! When we are forced to move beyond our ego, we suddenly make ourselves available to other sources of knowledge – to the Spirit.

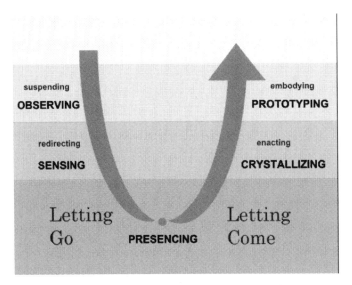

What Senge et al. describe as "presencing" is the experience of the coming in of the new and the transformation of the old. Once a group crosses this threshold, nothing remains the same. Individuals connect with both mind and heart.

When helping a golfer who has lost his swing, the master coach in the novel and film *The Legend of Bagger Vance* advises, "Seek it with your hands -- don't think about it, feel it. The wisdom in your hands is greater than the wisdom of your head will ever be." (Allied Filmworkers, 2000). Members and the group as a whole begin to operate with a heightened level of energy and sense of future possibility. They can begin to function as an intentional vehicle for the future that wants to emerge.

You've seen a herd of goats
going down to the water
The lame and dreamy goat brings up the rear.
There are worried faces about that one
but now they're laughing.
because look! as they return,
that goat is leading!
There are many different kinds of knowing,
The lame goat's is kind a branch
that leads back to the roots of presence.
Learn from the lame goat,
and lead the herd home. (Rumi, 2004)

Michael Finkel, writing in *The Atlantic Monthly*, describes Steven Allen, the British dry stone waller champion, competing on the Yorkshire moors.

I watched Allen work. He'd stand stock-still for a moment and stare at his wall with a calculating look. Then he would swiftly turn around and bend down and select a stone. He'd twist it and jiggle it and flip it over and back, as if fiddling with prayer beads. Then he'd pick up his hammer, hold the stone to his thigh, and chip off pieces with a few sharp taps. One of the qualities that sets Allen apart from other wallers is his feel for the hidden seams snaking through a rock ... When Allen hit a rock, it invariably fractured along a plane as smooth as a sail. (Finkel, 2000)

Equally impressive was Allen's speed. But it was speed that grew out of knowledge and focus, unlike the busy kind of speed we commonly observe around us. His speed grew from his ability to see emerging patterns. Far more often, in the pressure of leading change, speed grows from a place of impatience and insecurity, and when it does, what we build is not likely to stand for long. In fact, the moment we stop work, it's likely to collapse. Finkel writes, "If he was setting [the stone] into a space between two others, the rock would literally click into place, wedged between its neighbours as tightly and neatly as if Allen were building with Lego bricks. He'd nod, reach down and sweep up the chips he'd broken off, and pack them into the center of the wall. Then he'd study the next gap for a second or two, spin around, and pick up another stone" (Finkel, 2000).

Allen's speed was dependent on his perception of a larger pattern. He closed in on something, and then let it go. David Whyte writes that "the key seems to be to find a restful yet attentive presence in the midst of our work, to open up a spaciousness even in the center of our responsibility." (Whyte, 2001, p. 121).

It's critical that we find some other source of energy other than our own effort and will. Our constant efforts exhaust us and prevent us from creating something that endures. Whyte notes that a well-built, dry stone wall, free of cement, can settle and move and adapt to temperature and function for hundreds of years. In the limestone areas of Yorkshire there are walls dating to the twelfth century. As Finkel put it, "Cement walls do not reach old age. Cement walls do not move. They crack, and then they fall. 'Cement,' Allen says, 'is a sin.'" (Finkel, 2000).

At the source of the longest river
The voice of the hidden waterfall
And the children in the apple-tree
Not known, because not looked for
But heard, half-heard, in the stillness
Between two waves of the sea.
Quick now, here, now, always--
A condition of complete simplicity
(Costing not less than everything)

T.S. Eliot, "Little Gidding," V

Chapter 4

Crossing the Unknown Sea

Mount Everest and K2 are the two highest peaks in the world. Everest was first summited in 1953 and K2 in 1954. But the comparison ends there. While Everest is the highest mountain in the world by 237 meters, K2 is far more difficult to climb. By 2013 Everest had been summited nearly 7000 times, K2 barely 300 times.

K2 towers to 8,611 meters, or 28,251 feet above sea level. K2 is located on the China-Pakistan border between Baltistan, in the north of Pakistan, and the country of Xinjiang, China. It is the highest point of the Karakoram Range.

K2 is known as the savage mountain due to the extreme difficulty of ascent. It has the second-highest fatality rate among high mountains. With around 300 successful summits and 80 fatalities, about one person dies on the mountain for every four who summit.

The documentary, *K2: Siren of the* Himalaya, premiered at the Banff Mountain Film Festival in 2012. The film follows a group of climbers during their attempt in the summer of 2009 to climb. Director Dave Ohlson made the trek to climb K2 with elite alpinists Gerlinde Kaltenbrunner, Fabrizio Zangrilli, Jake Meyer and Chris Szymiec.

There are many reasons why the film is fascinating. Because the 2009 attempt occurs on the 100-year anniversary of the Duke of Abruzzi and Vittorio Sella's Italian expedition to the same peak in 1909, the filmmakers licensed rare archival footage to provide historical perspective. It and the lyrical commentary from Sella's journal add a magical quality to the film.

Moreover, these elite alpinists are a rare breed. None of them is using supplementary oxygen, so acclimatization is a necessity. They go down to go up - moving up and down between high camps in order to adapt to the low oxygen conditions. In the end, the ice and the weather defeat them all. None of the members of the three teams make the summit. But the differences among the team members, and their varied reflections on climbing, on mountains, and on risk are illuminating.

Near the end of the summer, one alpinist admits defeat. Jake Meyer has made it to 27,000 feet. But he's asking hard questions. Why is the next thousand feet of ice and snow so special? Is it worth his life? Jake is not exactly timid. When he was 21 years old, he became the youngest Brit to climb the Seven Summits after reaching the top of Mount Everest in 2005.

Fabrizio Zangrilli exhibits a different quality. He wants to reach the summit – it's a big dream. But it may not happen this year. He surrenders to the conditions of the mountain and the limits of his own body. He'll come back another day.

Similarly, Gerlinde Kaltenbrunner is philosophical. She had planned to summit, but now she adjusts her plan. She has already summited thirteen of the world's greatest mountains, all of them over 8,000 meters, and each time without supplementary oxygen. She seems confident, but also content to let it go for another season. The next year her climbing team mate, Fredrik Ericsson, will be killed on K2 in a fall. Yet she returns in 2011 and reaches the summit. She becomes the first woman to complete all fourteen so-called eight-thousanders without supplemental oxygen.

These alpinists may be crazy, but they are uniquely *awake*. They are aware that one wrong step, one bad decision at 7,000 or 8,000 metres can mean death. The challenge of edges is the challenge of wakefulness. Leaders accustomed to a sense of urgency and control learn to avoid the edges and live from more predictable spaces near to the center.

But edges have advantages that the centre lacks. When we live with edges we learn alertness. People who live near cliffs live with a heightened awareness of their surroundings. These are places with unpredictable winds, often on a slope. You can't wander there thoughtlessly. Edges force us to observe and to listen. They help us to cultivate an inward life and attentiveness.

Edges generate tension, and so they represent a liminal kind of experience. Edges are literally thresholds: boundaries between one world and another. The gift of liminal space is heightened awareness and the need to make choices. For this reason, some people become addicted to adventure.

Most of us prefer to sleep. We prefer to drift through life with minimal effort. We travel to Nicaragua and stay in a four-star hotel. We prefer the stance of the tourist to the pilgrim: traveling with heavy packs and the baggage of past choices and partially lived lives. We often think our deep fatigue results from too much to do. In reality, it often results from doing things that *are not ours to do*, and maintaining an outward identity that is not really ours at all. The burden of a false identity is exhausting, and the greater the fear that this is our truth, the more we run into frenetic activity to escape it.

The Adaptive Cycle

We are living at a time when much of the way we see and describe ourselves is under immense strain from the currents of change that swirl around us. Our old fixed, terrestrial ideas and the language to describe those ideas do not seem terribly well adapted to the fluidity of our new ocean world. We are being impacted in enormous ways... by the tides of ecological and technological change and the sudden realization that we inhabit a much more complex, intimate universe than we imagined. (Whyte, 2001, p. 59).

The church is a complex system, and potentially an adaptive system. Here I want to recall the aforementioned latter two phases in the adaptive cycle. (Gunderson, 2012. Kindle Location 167-176):

3. The release or omega (Ω) phase. A disturbance that exceeds the system's resilience breaks apart its web of reinforcing interactions. This could be the loss of a founding pastor, or a sudden decline in employment in the area, or increased competition for members, or a major shift in demographics. In an abrupt turnabout, the material and energy accumulated during the conservation phase is released. Resources that were tightly bound are transformed or destroyed as connections break and systemic controls weaken. The release of resources generates a creative element.

4. The renewal or alpha (α) phase. Following a disturbance, uncertainty rules. Feeble internal controls allow a system to lose or gain resources, but also allow novelty to appear. Small chance events have the opportunity to powerfully shape the future. Invention, experimentation, and re-assortment are the rule. Skills, experience, and expertise lost by individual groups may coalesce around new opportunities. Novelty arises in the form of new initiatives, creative ideas, and new people.

The release phase sounds exciting; but it's often experienced as a kind of death. When this happens in organizations, it means profound loss for many individuals. The church they have attended for thirty years closes its doors. The founding pastor, having rich connections with people, leaves after twenty years to attend a distant seminary. A major theological split occurs in a school and a professor is fired and supporters are angry and move their allegiance to other schools. "Resources that were tightly bound are transformed or destroyed as connections break…" (Gunderson, 2012. Kindle Location 168). The release phase can be immensely painful; there is no guarantee that something better is coming.

When change is manageable, we are facing a technical challenge, not an adaptive change. When we face an adaptive challenge, or when something is obviously broken, then we need to disturb the system and encourage novelty. We need to reconnect with the context, with one another, and become learners again.

Stable systems are not lacking change; but its type of change is predictable. Discontinuous change is another animal. Sometimes we call it *phase transition*. In discontinuous change, sudden shifts can happen that surprise us; structures that appear fixed and solid can collapse in a very short time.

Consider what happens to a bottle of water left in a freezer. The temperature gradually lowers. Nothing much happens for a long time. Then suddenly as the temperature approaches zero Celsius something amazing happens: tiny crystals form, and other crystals form around those crystals until there is a mass movement in the water as it goes from liquid to solid. This is discontinuous change.

With phase transition, a threshold is crossed where rather than more of the same occurring, something completely new happens. There's a sudden jump to a new state of reality. Moreover, discontinuous change can be triggered by small events. When we get close to a threshold a small step can carry us beyond it. We sometimes call this phenomenon a tipping point. Social movements have been launched at a tipping point, such as when a mass of people change their minds about something, or change their focus of attention. November 1989 in Berlin. Early 2011, the Arab Spring. Before this threshold point is reached change seems impossible, but suddenly the walls fall down.

When Bob Geldof decided to organize the 1985 Live Aid concert, he had an unusual experience. He found that its momentum increased faster than he could respond to it. Doors that had been impenetrable a short time earlier suddenly swung open.

This kind of experience points to a power that is outside our control. Its roots are in social dynamics and spontaneous connections. Geldof's efforts alone were not enough to produce the result, which was more like a tidal wave compared to the small stone he had tossed in the water. In complexity science this is called *emergence.*

Steven Johnson in his book *Emergence* describes a single-celled organism called slime mould. (Johnson, 2002). They are single-celled when food is plentiful, but multi-celled when food is in short supply. As multi-celled entities, they can travel quickly to new areas to search for food sources. When they are successful, they become single-celled again.

For many years it was thought that a particular pacemaker cell controlled this unusual ability. It was impossible to conceive of the alternative to centralized control: spontaneous order. But eventually a scientist named Evelyn Keller discovered that there were no pacemaker cells; there was no centralized control mechanism. In *Getting to Maybe*, (Westley, Zimmerman & Patton, 2006), the authors compare the mechanism to a furnace and a thermostat. When the room temperature nears a set threshold, the furnace shuts off and it only starts again when the temperature drops below another set level.

For slime moulds, each cell has its own thermostat and its own furnace. It knows when it is time to separate and time to come together. Rather than rely on a central controller to determine the nature of the food supply, the assessment is made by each cell. When several cells make the same decision, they cluster together, serving both their own interest and the interest of the collective.

It took years for this theory of slime mould behaviour to be accepted, because organizational science and leadership norms stood in the way. Everyone knew that a central, determined, all-knowing leader was the organizational path to success. The dominance of that map closed all other options. But that was yesterday. In the complex, connected world of today we need to leverage knowledge and networks because we don't know what we don't know. Margaret Wheatley writes,

We don't have to know the future in order to be prepared for it. Organizations and communities that learn to work together, that know how to learn together, that trust one another, and that become more expansive and inclusive, develop the capacity to deal with the unknown. They create a capacity for working and thinking together that enables them to respond quickly and intelligently to whatever the future presents. (Wheatley, 1999)

But we also need courage if we're going to surf the unknown sea. In 1966, a dyslexic sixteen-year-old boy dropped out of school. With the help of a friend, he started a magazine for students and made money by selling ads to local businesses. He ran the operation out of the crypt inside a local church.

Four years later, he was looking for ways to grow his small magazine and started selling mail order records to the students who bought the magazine. The records sold well and he built his first record store the next year. After two years of selling records, he decided to open his own recording studio.

He rented the recording studio out to local artists, including one named Mike Oldfield. In that small studio, Oldfield created his hit song, *Tubular Bells*, which became the new label's first release. It went on to sell over five million copies.

Over the next decade, the young man grew his record label by adding bands like the Sex Pistols and the Rolling Stones. He continued starting companies: an airline business, then trains, then mobile phones, and on and on. Eventually there were over four hundred companies under his direction. Today – in spite of his inexperience – he's a billionaire. His name is Sir Richard Branson. James Clear tells his story after a personal meeting with Branson in 2013. Then he drops the bomb and he writes, "If you want to summarize the habits of successful people into one phrase, it's this: successful people start before they feel ready." (Clear, 2012).

The Unimagined World

It took many years for Israel to realize that their lives in Egypt had become unmanageable. And then came the transition to the Promised Land. That went well, right?

Well, sort of. It took just a few days for Israel to get out of Egypt. It took forty years to get Egypt out of Israel. It wasn't possible to skip that part. Transition is a process of disentangling and unlearning. It's painful and uncomfortable, but it's necessary preparation to enter the unimaginable world.

On the one side, we let go of habits and values and patterns of action that are familiar and understood. These practices and values were not theoretical: they anchored our lives and gave them stability. Until we are well into the letting-go process we rarely realize just what is required of us. It feels intensely vulnerable.

On the other side, we pick up something new, or rediscover something we almost lost. We re-enter the narratives and traditions that anchor our lives in Christ. The Exodus story suddenly becomes *our* story; it becomes a personal narrative of transition, disentangling, and remembering. Entering the traditions of our faith helps us reconnect not just with God but with our faith community. Tradition becomes personal experience. The recovery of hours of prayer and of traditional practices of silence and reflection is not incidental to our time: it is a living movement to reconnect with God that is necessitated by liminal conditions.

In recent movies homeostasis – stability – is seen to be deadly. The *Divergent* series describes a utopian society built on the ruins of the old world. But the apparent stability is a manufactured stability, controlled by elites, where threats (difference) is quickly marginalized. The world begins to fall apart when *divergents* appear.

In long periods of cultural stability, organizations establish very particular roles and methods and ways of being. These conditions become set in cement and prevent us from observing key changes in the context. Cement is sin: it prevents an adaptive response.

"Generals lose new wars because they are still fighting old battles."[3]

It was 1981, and the engine in my 1965 Chev was burning oil. I decided I would do the minimal work and replace the rings, retool the valves and valve seats: a top-end job. I drove the car into my father's garage and used his trusty chain hoist to lift the eight-cylinder motor off the mounts. At the time I had no idea that the smooth running chain hoist had an unusual pedigree.

World War One was a nasty, brutal affair. It was a trench war, a defensive war, with fixed lines and little movement for years. There were many hard lessons, and after the war the French responded with the Maginot Line, a series of concrete fortifications built into the high ground along its border with Switzerland, Germany and Luxembourg. The line did not extend to the channel because of the French desire to avoid offending neutral Belgium. It was an engineering feat: layers of underground bunkers connected by underground tunnels. At the peak were large guns facing toward Germany. Power was provided by underground diesels. The network included recreation facilities, a library, and even a hospital and movie theatre.

The Maginot line was a conditioned response to a known problem: how to stop a sudden attack from Germany. Then along came a small man named Hitler who rewrote the rules. Hitler believed the key to success in war was shock and awe. He tooled a fast-moving army for a

---

[3] Overheard on CBC Radio, *Ideas*. April, 2007.

lightning war. When his generals encountered the fixed fortifications of the Maginot Line, they simply went north around the obstacle.

Not long after the war, around 1953, a Canadian corporal stationed in France was touring the French countryside. He and a friend had driven to one of the access points for the Maginot Line. The corporal was a diesel mechanic, and he wanted to have a look at the power-plant that was two levels down. They descended with the help of a flashlight. When they resurfaced they took with them a number of souvenirs, including a hardened steel chain hoist weighing about sixty-five pounds that my father used all his life.

Our successes often become a set-up for future failures, as happened to the French in 1940. The generals were trying to fight the First World War all over again. Germany, which had been defeated in 1918, had been in chaos forcing it to discard its old traditions and habits – good and bad – in favour of new ways of thinking.

In stable times habits and roles come to be seen not as chosen or embedded in a certain culture but as the way things *should be and should always be.* For much of the twentieth century organizations in North America functioned within a stable, well-managed, and relatively predictable environment. The assumptions of Modernity prevailed: by rational and technological means we could make and maintain our world. Our collective intelligence and know-how would help us attain the good life.

Since early in the last century, churches adopted the same way of seeing the world. This corporate form and imagination became embedded in our churches via the culture. Leadership roles and functions developed in this context to fit the needs of stable congregations. Pastors and church leadership learned these roles and ways of being as the normal way to run an effective church, and churches rewarded workers who were effective in these roles.

Around 1980 these assumptions began to erode as our culture began to seriously transition. Business leaders were the first to explore these changes and begin to adapt, but churches largely failed to see the writing on the wall. The following diagram, adapted from Plowman et al (2007, p. 341-356) suggests the scope of these changes.

Traditional Leaders	Complex Leaders
Minimize conflict & reduce uncertainty	Disrupt Existing patterns
Operate as controllers	Encourage novelty
Make decisions, direct order	Act as Sensemakers

Leadership in Emergent, Networked Conditions

In a stable culture traditional leadership functions effectively. Tasks are specialized and routinized, departments are divided by specialty and operate in silos. Centralized, top-down operations where information flows largely one way is workable when one can predict and control outcomes.

In today's new, connected, complex environment traditional leadership is dysfunctional. Networks are the new reality, representing not merely a new method but the way things really are. Relationality is

113

more fundamental than rationality.[4] In contrast to the centralized authority of the old world, networks may branch out from a common centre, or have no centre at all.

We need to be connected, and we need everyone contributing. In a British study in 2010, bees solved the classic "traveling salesman" problem faster than super-computers, which took days to solve it. The traveling salesman problem involves finding the shortest possible route between cities, visiting each city only once. Bees are the first animals to figure this out. According to Queen Mary University researchers, bees learn to fly the shortest possible route between flowers even if they find the flowers in a different order. But how is this possible?

Distributed intelligence. The power of the collective. Ants, bees, and termites, it turns out, are smarter than humans at some things. Non-linear interactions have the potential of generating an adaptive response. In a similar way networks leverage distributed intelligence. But there is a cost depending on how you engage. Hierarchy is efficient, but it concentrates power at the top. If you need total control, hierarchy is perfect. But if you want maximum adaptability, then you need more intelligence than a structure of command and control can offer. When you face complexity, you need a knowledge network.

The problem is, you can't control a network; you can only invite participation. This requires that power and authority are disentangled. But if authority doesn't reside in particular leaders, where does it reside? Christians have an easy answer: Jesus and the Spirit! Christians fondly recite this creed, but rarely practice it. What it means in practice is that we have to reconnect purpose and authority. It's all about the mission. We'll return to this in the next chapter.

---

[4] Newbigin wrote that "Interpersonal relatedness belongs to the very being of God. Therefore, there can be no salvation for human beings except in relatedness." *The Open Secret* (Grand Rapids: Eerdmans, 1990) 70.

Rather than representing an organizational machine, networks expand organically. Leaders who are effective in networks are less like managers, and more like gardeners who plant, prune, cultivate and harvest. In this complex environment *means* are secondary to connection. Frances Hesselbein, for one, "banned the hierarchy and, involving many heads and hands, built a new kind of structure. The new design took people out of the boxes of the old hierarchy and moved them into a more circular, flexible and fluid management system that released the energy and the spirit of our people" (Hesselbein, 2002, p. 3). This organization built dispersed and diverse leadership, and distributed leadership to the edges in order to unleash the potential of the system.

The shift from predictability and control to distributed and complex requires a shift in the way leaders *are*, not just in what they do. That's a difficult demand, but a hopeful one, because adaptive leadership is dynamic, and those who master its demands are lousy at maintaining institutions, but pretty good at generating movement. Long before our faith was an institution, it was a dynamic, living movement. As we move further into the twenty-first century, and as our institutions fail, we have the opportunity to discover something older.

Harlan Cleveland was a competent leader and a futurist. As the world changed around him, he is engaging in thinking about the implications of leadership in the unimaginable world. In his book *Nobody In Charge*, he lists eight attitudes that he believes are indispensable to the management of complexity.

- A lively intellectual curiosity; an interest in everything – because everything really is related to everything else.
- A genuine interest in what other people think and why they think that way – which means you have to be at peace with yourself.

- A feeling of special responsibility for envisioning a future that's different from a straight-line projection of the present.
- A hunch that most risks are not there to be avoided but to be taken.
- A mindset that crises are normal, tensions can be promising and complexity is fun.
- A realization that paranoia and self-pity are reserved for people who don't want to be leaders.
- A sense of personal responsibility for the general outcome of your efforts.
- A quality of optimism – the conviction that there must be a better outcome possible than that which results from adding up all the expert advice. (Cleveland, 2002, p. 119)

Crossing the Unknown Sea

In chapter one we saw how the Franklin expedition took the habits and customs of their world with them. The burden of the past killed them. Despite their brave commitment to explore a way through the Northwest Passage, they carried the assumptions of their nineteen-century world.

The baggage we bring with us that we expect will serve us just as well tomorrow is like the china plates and library books that shaped Franklin's imagination. They don't help us create a new world: they only prevent us from leaving the familiar past behind.

But compare Franklin's mindset with the 1905 expedition of Roald Amundsen. (Brannen, 2016). In a ship roughly a tenth the size of Franklin's, Amundsen's successful journey to the North Pole was almost boring. He abandoned the technology and the assumptions of British society, and spent years learning from those who knew the most about survival in the Arctic. He adopted the clothing and hunting techniques of the Inuit. Rather than face nature head on with the goal of dominance, he submitted to it humbly and flexibly. His ability to submit to an adaptive challenge ensured his success.

Now consider the people of Israel. They endured captivity in Egypt for four hundred years. When God sent Moses to lead them out, he arrived with no map. And yet he would be Israel's guide through some of the toughest geography in the world. Why not simply give them a map? There are at least two reasons.

First, God himself wanted to be the way forward. He wanted a people radically dependent on his Spirit. Second, the process was as important as the destination. God wasn't just providing deliverance. He wasn't a substitute for a standing army. *He's the King!* He is forming a people for himself, a people who mirror his own heart. Eric Hoffer gives us a hint toward the difference. "Moses wanted to turn a tribe of enslaved Hebrews into free men. You would think that all he had to do was to gather the slaves and tell them that they were free. But Moses knew better. He knew that the transformation of slaves into free men was more difficult and painful than the transformation of free men into slaves . . ." (Hoffer, 1969, May 20)

Third, Moses was not a map reader. He was a navigator. Map readers and navigators are actually two different *kinds* of people. While it is possible for map readers to become navigators, it's not easy, and many won't make the transition. Map readers as leaders make good managers; navigators as leaders are explorers. Map readers love stability; navigators enjoy the wilderness. Map readers are impatient with process; navigators embrace the journey. Map-reading is a lonely vocation; navigators value company. Navigators are creative, adaptive leaders.

Navigation is both an old skill and an ancient metaphor. John Climacus uses the Greek word *kubernetes* in his early seventh-century book *Ladder of Divine Ascent.* The word means pilot, helmsman, or guide, and he used it to speak of spiritual direction. When a ship is entering a harbour universal knowledge is no longer adequate; local knowledge becomes critical. The pilot comes alongside the captain and crew to guide them safely through unfamiliar waters, past hidden obstacles. Travelling in a straight line in unknown waters can get you killed.

When Moses led God's people out of Egypt it would be easy to imagine he was leading a journey from Point A to Point B. That simply was not the case. Moses was not really leading people at all; he was following the Lord, and leading a process whereby God could form a ragtag mob into one people, following the Spirit.

When we helped to plant Metro, a church in the urban core of Kelowna, the mother church was entering a crisis. The Metro community and ministry were growing rapidly. With more than fifty per cent of our community either homeless or in addiction, the needs were endless. How would we hire staff? The mother church could not help. We sought individual donors who saw the vision, and we began building bridges of collaboration to other agencies. New partnerships would provide stable funding. Today Metro is a hybrid: it looks like an agency from the outside, but like a faith community from the inside. Metro is a novelty within the denomination, but may be its future.

How do we begin to cultivate navigators? By practicing the skills of *kubernetes*, skills that represent a response to adaptive challenges. Some of these practices are:

- create a context where problems invoke possibilities;
- find or create rituals that invoke memory (an internal location);
- initiate and convene conversations that shift peoples experience – help people ask new questions and then like a poet give them new language;
- value and affirm process, get comfortable with mystery;
- value experimentation and risk, cultivate generosity; and
- listen and pay attention.

But to apprehend
The point of intersection of the timeless
With time, is an occupation for the saint —
No occupation either, but something given
And taken, in a lifetime's death in love,
Ardour and selflessness and self-surrender.

T.S. Eliot, "The Dry Salvages," V

We shall not cease from exploration
And the end of all our exploring
Will be to arrive where we started
And know the place for the first time.

T.S. Eliot, "Little Gidding," V

Chapter 5

Listening for the Future

We don't have to know the future in order to be prepared for it. Organizations and communities that learn to work together, that know how to learn together, that trust one another, and that become more expansive and inclusive, develop the capacity to deal with the unknown. They create a capacity for working and thinking together that enables them to respond quickly and intelligently to whatever the future presents. (Spears, 2001).

Experimental psychologist Richard Nisbett dates his curiosity about the relationship of culture to perception to a debate he had with a Chinese graduate student in the early 1990s. He realized that there were fundamental differences in the way the two cultures thought. The reason? "The Chinese believe in constant change," his student told him. 'Westerners live in a more deterministic world. They think they can control events because they know the rules that govern the behavior of objects." (Ramo, 2009, p. 155).

In the East change is seen as a constant. In the West we lean toward determinism, even through a religious lens (For example, God upholds the universe and creates laws which make interactions predictable). But think how differently these two cultures approach problem-solving! In the East, one must pay constant attention to shifting conditions and to the complex relationship between variables. The emphasis is on context, a relational and more-or-less *gestalt* approach to reality. In the West, we look at the whole through the parts, and we believe that a knowledge of the parts grants us understanding of the whole. Moreover, we seek a very special kind of knowledge aimed at granting us power and control.[5]

Nisbett designed a test to measure the focal interest of Eastern and Western students. Thirty-six images flashed every thirty seconds as an eye-tracker recorded where the subject looked. Western students immediately looked at the foreground object -- the horse or tiger, for example. And once they spotted the central image they spent the bulk of the time looking right at it. Chinese students, by contrast, looked at the environment first, probing the complex background of forest or field. They did look at the focal object, but for far less time than the American students.

In the West the cult of individual power shapes our approach to reality. We are less interested in relationships than in the power relations between players, and we are most interested in the central player, because that's where we believe the real power lies. The tiger in one image took up twenty-five per cent of the screen but captured eighty per cent of the attention of the Western students. Nisbett later reversed the trick, wondering if Western students would notice a change in the background. What if the horse stayed the same but the field around it went from autumn to spring flowers? Most of the Western subjects missed the shift. An ancient Sufi teaching captures the difference: "You think because you understand *one* you must

---

[5] Heidegger distinguished between meditative knowing and calculative knowing. The latter distorts the subject because it asks primarily power questions. In physics the problem is *indeterminacy*.

understand *two*, because one and one makes two. But you must also understand *and*." (Meadows, 1982, p. 98-108).

This leads to two critical conclusions. First, relationships are not just *interesting*, they are the shape of reality. We cannot know the whole through the parts. One physicist, Henry Stapp, describes elementary particles as, "in essence, a set of relationships that reach outward to other things." (Capra, 1983, p. 81). We give names to individual particles, but they are only intermediate states in a network of interactions.

Second is the importance of local knowledge. It is in local connections, our relationship to the context, that our future is hidden. I say hidden, because the important information is not always obvious. As Nisbett discovered, we pay attention to what our mental maps tell us is important.

Some years ago, a researcher at Harvard Medical School presented a group of radiologists a series of x-ray images, used to spot cancer nodules in human lungs. He asked them what they saw. The radiologists did a great job at spotting the tiny cancer nodules that an untrained eye would overlook.

But these weren't ordinary images. An image of a man in a gorilla suit shaking his fist had been superimposed on the x-rays. Fewer than one in five of the radiologists *saw* it. The problem was in the way their brains were so narrowly fixed on what they were doing (looking for cancer nodules), that the gorilla became essentially invisible to them. We develop mental maps as aids in orienting ourselves in a complex world. But as we saw with Ken Killip, those maps can get us killed. "Environments are not passive wrappings, but are rather active processes which are invisible. The ground rules, pervasive structure, and overall patterns of environments elude easy perception" (Mcluhan & Fiore, 2001, p. 68).

This is why contextualization is so important: we need to pay attention to the interdependency between how things appear and how the environment causes them to appear. How do we find the information that is critical to our adaptation? How can we remain sensitive to the information we may otherwise miss because we went looking only for the information we found? One of the keys is participation, and we'll talk more about this in chapter 6.

The Importance of Local Knowledge

Christian leaders in the West have noted that the party is over. We are no longer the dominant force in culture: we have entered post-Christendom, and even a *post-Christian* phase. Partly in response to this new reality, the buzz word among change leaders and future oriented thinkers has been *missional*. But the framing of this shift has been less clear. Do we believe that the church needs to return to the centre of our culture? Or are we better off on the margins, which is where the church existed when she spread like wildfire in the first two centuries? In *The Age of the Unthinkable* Ramo quotes Louis Halle, the American strategist of the 1950s who observed that foreign policy "is made not in reaction to the world but in reaction to an image of the world in the minds of the people making decisions. (Ramo, 2009, p. 13). It depends in part on how we understand the landscape.

Alan Roxburgh has noted that we continually ask church-centered questions of God's mission. But it is not God's church that has a mission in the world; rather, *God's mission has a church in the world.* It is God's mission and God's kingdom, that have priority. Yet our gaze has continually been fixed on the church. As a consequence we continue to shrink God's work to fit within the constraints of our buildings and programs. Moreover, and even more damaging, is we shrink God himself to those dimensions. How do we correct our faulty perspective? How do we learn to ask new questions? How do we recover a kingdom perspective? (Roxburgh, 2015)

It starts by getting quiet. In the introduction to his volume on local theology, Clemens Sedmak writes that "theology is about mindfulness." He notes, "Doing theology is a way of listening to God. God's voice is often a whisper. God's presence is hidden. Theology asks for an attitude of attentiveness, awareness, mindfulness... Theology reads the book of the world, looking 'in between the lines'" (Sedmak, 2002, p. 6).

Our culture and technologies are becoming immensely fragmented. There may be more demands for our attention than at any time in history. We belong to multiple communities, and we are never beyond the reach of our cell phones. These technologies enhance our connectivity but not our belonging, and they mitigate against our being fully present where we are. Yet apart from that presence we have little hope of enriching our commitment to live locally; and without that commitment, our knowledge of the local remains superficial. Sedmak argues that waking up involves going to the roots of the matter. It is a refusal to accept easy answers, a quick diagnosis. Moreover, it is sensitive to the conditions of ordinary people and ordinary life.

When complexity theory was gaining traction the operation of DNA was mostly understood. What was unclear was how that global blueprint was enacted locally. How does an undifferentiated cell know that it should become an ear, and not a tongue or an eye? Observations from the lives of ants offered a possible answer via swarm theory. How do ants, without any centralized control, decide where to look for food or where to discard their waste? They look to what their neighbours are doing. Individually ants are stupid; collectively they are powerfully intelligent.

Similarly, cells figure out what signals to pay attention to by connecting to cells around them. Gerald Edelman calls this process *topobiology*, from the Greek word for place, '*topos*.' Cells rely heavily on the code of DNA for development, but they need a sense of place to work effectively. It turns out that the DNA code is worthless apart from the cell's knowledge of the overall picture, a task that is accomplished "by the elegant strategy of paying attention to one's neighbour." (Johnson, 2001, p. 86).

Doing local theology, "making sense" is not the sole province of professionals, even though it has been on loan to them. Being awake in a world of wonder is the privilege of children. How do we adults recover that early awareness? Our local knowledge must be a different kind of knowing than that which we can gain through scientific detachment. Knowledge that is transformative requires participation. St. Thomas Aquinas wrote that "we know things better through love than through knowledge." Part of our requirement will be a new appreciation for the particularity of place.[6]

The Beauty of Presence

> There is a way between voice and presence
> where information flows.
> In disciplined silence it opens.
> With wandering talk it closes. (Rumi & Barks, 2004).

Paying attention is a communal task, and the challenge of presence is the challenge of dual-knowing, just like seeing with two eyes creates a single image. Seeing with one eye, the image is flat. Seeing with both eyes creates a three-dimensional image, an image of life. In the same way that two eyes create one image, we need to see with both mind and heart: we need *wholesight.*

This dual knowing can help us to move beyond the limits of the modern, scientific paradigm.[7] We need to know the world as a sacred space, the temple that God indwells. When we're attentive to God, and

---

[6] In this connection see my earlier work, *No Home Like Place* (Portland: Urban Loft, 2014).

[7] The objectification of the world has been of particular interest in the study of phenomenology. The work of Merleau-Ponty and Husserl has given us a world between the objective and subjective ones.

126

attentive to the place we inhabit, we become present with God and for his kingdom. Our mission is *shalom*, to work with God in setting the world to rights. The authors of *The New Parish* call this movement "faithful presence" (Sparks, Soerens & Friesen, 2014, p. 86ff). We become present with people in the neighbourhood for the sake of the kingdom. We contextualize the gospel with our bodies, resulting in a different *kind* of knowledge. We are not analytically detached, but rather we are part of the fabric of the community.

Becoming present (incarnate) in the neighbourhoods to which we are sent allows us to know the community in the most personal and relational sense. The problem with an exegetical approach to the neighbourhood is the problem of detachment. As Paul Virilio put it, "We now have the possibility of seeing at a distance, of hearing at a distance, and of acting at a distance, and this results in a process of de-localization, of the unrooting of the being... Our contemporaries will henceforth need two watches: one to watch the time, the other to watch the place where one actually is" (Virilio & Oliveira, 1996).

Too true. My smart phone tracks my actual location for my friends even as I detach myself from my physical space while I check my mail. I can be with people, but not present to them, and technology magnifies this problem for us constantly. The problem with virtual space is that it is *not* connected to the particularities of place. Yet it is precisely place that generates the unique conditions of life. *To be is to be placed*. As Einstein's teacher, Hermann Minkowski, said: "Nobody ever noticed a place except at a time, or a time except at a place."[8] But our detachment from place is part of the problem; our detachment from one another feeds the huge gap in belonging.

---

[8] Source unknown.

Presence, belonging, shalom: that's our *telos,* our mission. Jean Vanier writes, "The mission of a community is to give life to others, that is to say, to transmit new hope and new meaning to them. Mission is revealing to others their fundamental beauty, value and importance in the universe, their capacity to love, to grow and to do beautiful things and to meet God." (Vanier, 1989).

But this means engaging down in the dirt, among ordinary people and their issues. It means not just knowing, but becoming *known*. It means engaging in the politics of cities and neighbourhoods, working for the common good. It means getting rooted richly until we know in our guts what the important issues are, including those that work *against* shalom – against rich belonging, against justice and peace. No wonder Newbigin writes, "I do not think that the geographical parish can ever become irrelevant or marginal. There is a sense in which the primary sense of neighbourhood must remain primary, because it is here that men and women relate to each other simply as human beings and not in respect of their functions in society." (Newbigin, 1981, p. 64)

Theologians have given us rich volumes of works examining the characteristics of God, and the inner life of the Trinity. These works are important and have helped us to understand who God is, and consequently who we are and how we should live. But now we need theologians of the ordinary places. We need theology that explores how civic design impacts human relationships, and how it impacts our ability to imagine such things as transcendence. We need theology that examines issues of mobility and rootedness, dislocation and belonging, exclusion and inclusion. We need theology that considers how the urban spaces invite us to rest and connect with others, or invite us to detach and to move on. We need theology that examines issues of race and gender relative to *shalom*. We need theology that considers our methods of transportation and their ability to further fragment us or separate us from the places we live.

In other words, becoming present in our neighbourhoods is an issue for practical theology as well as for spiritual formation. And ordinary believers are going to have to learn to do every-day theology. While this seems like a daunting task, it is really the task of each new generation. It's just that the task is made more urgent when the structures and models we have relied on are failing us.

In his primer on theology, Karl Barth tells the story of a series of lectures he gave in the post-war ruins of the *Kurfürsten* castle in Bonn, Germany. A rebuilding project was underway. In the summer of 1946 Barth began his lectures. Every morning at seven they met to sing a psalm or a hymn to cheer each other up. By eight o'clock, "the rebuilding of the quadrangle began to advertise itself in the rattle of an engine as the engineers went to work to restore the ruins" (Barth, 1959). Barth notes that this is where we accomplish vigorous theological work—in the ruins of an old world in hope of creating the new. Unlearning – deconstruction – opens the way for new work, and new learning. It takes effort, and it's usually messy.

The Story of SEMCO

In the late 1980s a young Brazilian businessman named Ricardo Semler took over his family's thirty-three year-old marine equipment company, Semco. Brazil in the 1980s was enduring a period of hyper-inflation: in a good year prices would double. In 1990 prices rose more than 1,000 percent. According to Semler running a business in Brazil was like riding a bull during an earthquake. "Some of the worst jolts come not from the bull but from the landscape" (Ramo, 2009, p. 246).

Semco was one of the best engineering firms in Brazil, with customers spread as far as Los Angeles and Oslo. But the quality of their work was no protection against the economic earthquakes. Just borrowing capital to finance orders required a premium of thirty percent over the rate of inflation. Between 1990 and 1994, one in every four Brazilian manufacturing firms went under.

Semler felt tremendous pressure to sustain the business. He consulted American business schools; it didn't help. He reorganized using a Japanese management system. That attempt likewise failed. When the government decided to seize the bank accounts of most Brazilians in 1990, Semler and his managers met with employees one hundred at a time to admit they had come up empty. There were two options left: cut salaries, which made an impossible situation worse, or sacrifice some workers to save the rest. They were looking desperately for a third way out. Finally some employees proposed an alternative. They would accept pay cuts in exchange for three things: a larger share of profits; a forty per cent pay cut for Semler and the management team; and a member of their union co-signing every cheque. Semler decided they had nothing to lose.

Within two months, Semco was running at breakeven. To save money, employees started handling work the firm had been contracting out. They served as security guards and janitors and helped cook in the cafeteria. For four or five months the company made a profit in the worst times they had ever seen. When the Brazilian economy began to recover, the managers at Semco knew they could return to business as usual, but they knew they had witnessed a miracle. They had seen an explosion of energy, enthusiasm, and flexibility. Semler wondered: was there a way to run the business permanently with a new set of rules?

Instead of running on traditional policies, Semco invented a free-for-all corporation. He wanted as little structure and management as possible. Most of the employees became independent contractors. They set their own salaries and working hours. The firm was broken into tiny pieces, with no work unit comprising more than a hundred employees. Semco workers decided for themselves how and when they would produce new products – and how much they would charge for them. The productivity of Semco increased four hundred per cent. When a group of engineers asked Semler if they could take a pay cut to create time to look around for new projects in exchange for a share of the profits, it soon became the company's fastest growing group. By the time the system was fully functional Semler observed, "no one really knows how many people we employ." Semco became one of the fastest-growing companies in Brazil.

Semco's best businesses were ones that employees invented themselves in response to some opportunity they saw at the ground level. Over time these were more successful than any created via strategic planning. Bad ideas withered quickly, while good ones blossomed and expanded. Semco looked increasingly less like a business organization and more like an immune system. Its knowledge was everywhere; control was radically decentralized; its reaction time to a changed environment was profoundly quick.

Organisms that survive through periods of rapid change develop acute sensory feedback systems. These abilities are structured into the organism in very careful ways. With the human body, we have touch, taste, hearing and sight on the macro level. On the micro level we have a powerful immune system. On the systemic level we have particular gifts. Prophets are people with a special sensitivity to the Spirit. Pastors have a special sensitivity to relational and system dynamics. But no one monopolizes discernment: it seems spread through the body, and it is keyed to a communal process.

Discernment is a core practice for churches in a new environment. Ruth Haley Barton defines discernment as "an ever-increasing capacity to 'see' or discern the work of God in the midst of the human situation so that we can align ourselves with the work God is doing." (Barton, 2011, p. 20). Barton lists five foundational beliefs related to discernment.

1. Spiritual discernment, by definition, takes place in and thru the Trinity.
2. The impulse to discern—to want to respond to the leading of the Spirit – is itself a good spirit that needs to be cultivated.
3. It requires a deep belief – *confidence* – in the goodness of God.

4. It grows from a conviction that love is our ultimate calling.
5. It requires a commitment to doing the will of God as it is revealed to us – surrender.

Discernment is a quality of attentiveness to God that develops over time as an ability to sense God's heart and purpose. It requires us to "test the spirits," and is a spiritual practice (like all of them) that opens us to the activity of God beyond what we can do for ourselves. (Barton, 2011, p. 57-62). This means asking good questions – questions that open space for a new imagination. And it means cultivating solitude as space for listening. The more this task is understood as a communal responsibility, the more likely that an adaptive response will be made.

The Church Art of Listening

I've always been fascinated by wheels; particularly old wheels. It may be the paradox of frozen movement; it may be non-linearity and the connection of past and future; perhaps I am reminded of the essential nature of life as change. I'm not sure all what attracts me to wheels, but Henri Nouwen shares a similar attraction. He writes, "These wheels help me understand the importance of a life lived from the centre. When I move along the rim, I can reach one spoke after the other, but when I stay at the hub, I am in touch with all the spokes at once" (Nouwen, 1983)

Have you ever sat beside a still pool? A still pool is not really motionless; just consider the speed at which the earth is rotating! A still pool is not without motion, but it is *radically sensitive*. The slightest breeze sends ripples running across its surface. Throw a pebble into the pool, and the reaction is instant. The surface is disturbed, and the rings spread outward from the centre to the edges. TS Eliot, fond of paradox, writes,

Words move, music moves
Only in time; but that which is only living

Can only die. Words, after speech, reach
Into the silence. Only by the form, the pattern,
Can words or music reach
The stillness, as a Chinese jar still
Moves perpetually in its stillness. (Eliot, 1960)

Stillness is not inaction: rather, it is an intention toward openness. Stillness allows us to tune our inner ears to a new level of attention. Formation is all about attention. Our appetites distract us; we pursue the wrong things. Our culture distracts us, noise pulls our attention away from God and Spirit. We are attracted and distracted: to flash and show, to posturing and bluster, to things of little substance, so that we are continually attentive to the wrong things. But "God has made foolish the wisdom of this world." (1 Cor 1:20). How then do we learn to attend to the right things? Silence can be our teacher.

Dwelling in silent places, however, is not an easy task. Few of us choose it, yet many of us find ourselves there. God usually has to engineer the journey. Someone we trusted fails us; a job we counted on suddenly ends; a child or spouse dies; we are struck blind on the road to Emmaus. Once we arrive at our destination, we are disinclined to call it home. This is why spiritual directors and counselors are often sought in times of transition; we need outward support and encouragement to endure liminal space. On our own we tend to run for security, back to the familiar gardens of Egypt.

Listening begins as a priestly task and then becomes prophetic and poetic. It begins in a quiet and personal space and then becomes communal and incarnational. It connects what was with what will be. Not content with the status quo, with a tame God and a civil religion, it reaches forward in hope and faith to God's surprising future. Far from merely the task of some designated leader, this is a communal process. We empty ourselves of our personal agendas and wait together to hear God speaking. We enter the pregnancy of a shared silence, a sacred space where the word can resound. It requires weakness more than strength, and surrender more than control. It requires vulnerability comparable to the kenotic vulnerability of Jesus, the Word who became flesh among us.

We react to silence in the same way we react to emptiness: with fear of the unknown, with a desire for control. We rightly lean toward purpose: emptiness invites us to postpone purpose and postpone meaning. Jacques Derrida argues that this kind of emptiness is a function of language that we have forgotten. He wrote that "complete meaning is always *postponed* in language; there is never a moment when meaning is complete and total." (Derrida, 1968). Derrida coined a new word: *différance*. He notes that difference is neither a word, nor a concept. Words and concepts are themselves *différance* from other words and concepts and this gives *différance* its meaning. Derrida explained like this:

The word "house" derives its meaning more as a function of how it differs from "shed", "mansion", "hotel", "building", "hovel", "hours", "hows", "horse", etc. etc., than how the word "house" may be tied to a certain image of a traditional house. Not only are the differences between the words relevant here, but the differentials between the images signified are also covered by *différance*. Deferral also comes into play, as the words that occur following "house" in any expression will revise the meaning of that word, sometimes dramatically so.

Thus, complete meaning is always *postponed* in language; there is never a moment when meaning is complete and total. (Derrida, 1968)

If complete meaning is always postponed, then it is always coming into being and never simply here or there. (Can you hear echoes of Jesus teaching on the kingdom of God in Luke 17:20-21?) Until recently we assumed that leadership was decisive, always clear, measurable, and always advancing. Compare this Western bias to this statement by Lao Tzu: *A good traveler has no fixed plans and is not intent on arriving.*

Perhaps leadership, then, is less about progress and more about process. Somehow leaders are attuned to difference and perhaps to becoming. Leadership is somehow anchored in the future as much as in the present.

Leadership is a communal function. A community that is connected to its context has many diverse points of connection. Individual leaders will always be limited. But leaders who are richly connected to their community may act like a hub in a network: enabling rich connection, and attuned to difference. "The 'church art' of listening to the whole and creating space for the new is leadership at its best." (Morse, 2012, p. 149).

An image of listening that moves me is the Very Large Array in Sirocco, New Mexico, featured in the movie *Contact*. The Array consists of twenty-seven independent radio antennae, all pointed at the heavens, collecting huge amounts of information via radio waves. Not all the information they collect is useful. In a sense, what determines the utility or even meaning of the information they collect is the question they are assigned to address. The lens that focuses the information, allowing it to make a difference, might be an individual or a team leading a particular project.

This analogy unlocks a rich perspective. If we begin with many sources - many "listeners" or collectors – then the field of information expands also. Sally Morgenthaler writes, "Groups that are too much alike find it harder to keep learning because each member is bringing less and less to the table. Homogeneous groups are great at doing what they do well, but they become progressively less able to investigate alternatives . . ." (Morgenthaler, 2007, p.183). The many are what give the system its great potential. The Array's twenty-seven lenses give it incredible listening power or "resolution" that two or three large dishes alone would lack.

Many listeners means high participation. Data is often lost to us not because it's not available, but because we don't have enough listeners attuned to the conditions. One or two listeners, in shifting and complex conditions, is simply not enough. With few listeners we lack a rich connection to the context, and thus we are also lacking needed knowledge.

Recovering a Leadership *Communitas*

One of the challenges leaders in organizations have faced is the dependence and passivity that grow when there is a lack of participation in the decision-making process. If I am shaped by a culture that says that only the strongest voices should participate, or only those with certain letters after their name, I am more likely to withhold my gifts or to use them in a very narrow frame. "I'm only the bookkeeper," or, "I'm only the janitor." A culture of participation, many listeners and many voices, becomes critical when an adaptive response is needed.

This corresponds with how we understand quantum reality. If organizational data is imagined as a wave function moving through space, then as it progresses, the potential interpretations expand. But when the wave meets a single observer, it collapses into one interpretation, responding to the conditions of measurement. At that moment all other potentials disappear and are lost. It is the single interpretation or event that is then passed down to others in the organization. The observation is presented as objective and the information as complete. Yet in the quantum world, this isn't possible. This was demonstrated clearly by Heisenberg (uncertainty) as well as by Schrodinger (his imagined cat).

Now imagine the information wave spreading out broadly into the organization. Instead of collapsing into one or a few interpretations, there are many moments of meeting – many events. At each intersection between observer and data, an interpretation appears that is specific to that observation. The potentials within the wave thus offer a richness of perspective that would otherwise be lost. The organization now has opportunity to select from a range of interpretations that mesh more closely with current and future conditions. This is a special kind of "sense-making" which we will examine more closely in the next chapter.

One possible objection to this description is the fear that the information flow would be overwhelming – the proverbial "fire-hose." This is where other actions come into play: discernment, intention, difference, and telos   the end goal. Leadership is a function of context and telos. Leadership is conditioned both by the need of the moment and the place we want to end up. In this sense leadership is always future-oriented. But furthermore, leadership must be attuned to difference.

Gregory Bateson helped us wrestle with the concept of *in*-formation. To be *in*-formed is to be inwardly formed. Leadership, like lenses, makes a difference. By choosing attention - and sometimes shifting focus - leadership disturbs a system, bringing change. "Leaders are to a social system what a properly shaped lens is to light. They focus intention and do so for better or for worse. If adaptive intention is required, the social system must be disturbed in a profound and prolonged fashion. Magnifying a threat or utilizing organizational devices to propagate 'genetic diversity' then becomes important." (Pascale, Milleman, Gioja, 2000, p. 140)

In *The Missional Leader* Roxburgh and Romanuk describe the role of leadership in our time: "to cultivate environments wherein the Spirit of God may call forth and unleash the missional imagination of the people of God." (Roxburgh and Romanuk, 2006, p. 75). This is one promise of a leadership community: connecting to our need to reimagine ourselves as missionaries in the post-Christendom culture we live in. One of the theses of this book is that special demands are made of our faith communities in these transitional times.

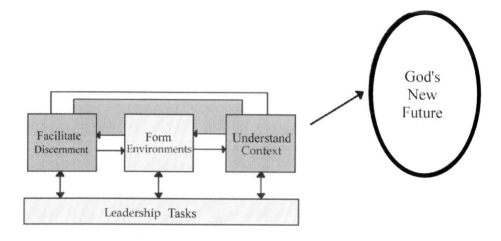

Four Requirements for Renewal

In these special conditions, there are at least four requirements for renewal. The first requirement is to recover a missional imagination. Missional imagination always precedes missional practice. The danger is that we pass too quickly over the needed theological work and remain merely pragmatists: a dynamic that has contributed to our loss of imagination and this current crisis. Part of this task is a poetic task: the creation of new language. As Len Sweet has noted, when the root metaphors change, so does everything else. The imaginative architecture of the modern world has collapsed. (Sweet, 2001).

The second requirement is to recover missional leadership. The church has largely marginalized the gifts that offer her an alternate vision of her future. Alan Hirsch and Alan Roxburgh have jointly pointed us back to Ephesians 4 and the apostolic team within Paul's view (Hirsch, 2006). We marginalized certain gifts when the church in modernity exchanged leadership for management. In the stable environment that has now passed away – the Christendom experiment – management and "tweaking the system" were often enough. Yet wherever the church is recovering the dynamic of a missional movement new leadership types are active.

The third requirement is to create an interpretive community. The immediate need is to produce local theologians; but secondly the need is for "communities of practice," which is both an embodied apologetic (the church as the true hermeneutic of the gospel) and a new social reality. But this community cannot exist apart from the communal reality of the Table, or the practice of "binding and loosing." I'll say a little about this here and then examine some new leadership types.

An interpretive community is needed for two reasons. First, when foundations shift we are pushed to ask new questions, and to approach Scripture afresh. Much of the work done in the last century was done in reaction to secularism, and much of it was done in response to foundations that no longer exist. Moreover, it was done as a privileged elite within the edifice of Christendom, and it was done without regard to context, in the assumption that every investigation and application would have universal validity.[9] But theology from a place of privilege and power was theology that often resulted in compromises for the sake of maintaining a place of privilege, while a disregard for context resulted in theology that was both colonial and patriarchal. Now that the edifice of Christendom is falling down, we have an opportunity to do theological work that is not self-protective: not primarily concerned with privilege or power, but that has the character of the one who humbled himself and gave everything on the Cross.

The invitation of the Spirit in this location is to enter a clearing together, and together to become faithful listeners. Walter Brueggemann observes that it was as the people of God went into exile

---

[9] See in particular the work of Michel de Certeau. A wonderful exploration of the meaning of place with regard to the gospel is given in *God Next Door: Spirituality and Mission in the Neighborhood* (Melbourne: Acorn Press, 2008)

that their imaginations were renewed (Brueggemann, 1997). They were forced to rethink much that they thought was clear; they went back to the text and listened anew to the Spirit. They did not see the extent of their own compromise until they were removed from a secure place— it seems we learn little until we are forced into liminality.

Moreover, we need an interpretive community because "truth" is not what it used to be. Whereas modernity still largely saw truth as an objective reality, now truth is largely a tribal reality. The solvents of individualism, romanticism and consumer culture leave us with only an appeal to truth that we can see and touch: truth must be embodied.[10] Truth that is storied in tradition, an appeal to truth beyond our subjective experience because it is anchored in history, also remains a source of appeal.

The fourth requirement is to distinguish between the church as an organism and the church as an institution. As far back as 1978 Howard Snyder was making this distinction, but it existed in the conversation of German theology long before as *Geselleschaft* and *Gemeinschaft.* Snyder explored the distinction more thoroughly in 1983 in *Liberating the Church,* arguing that our dominant metaphors have shaping power. Whether we choose a mechanistic image or an organic image influences the kind of community we are. Snyder writes that, "as man and woman become like their gods, so they become like their models. A machine model (a technosystem) produces human robots; an organic model (an ecosystem) produces healthy persons." (Snyder, 1983, p. 43).

---

[10] Of course this is a movement beyond the "intersubjectivity" of Husserl, but it is also distinct from the positivism that characterized Modernity.

The church exists in this world as *both* a living body and an institution. In systems language, the church has both designed structures and emergent structures. This is true for every human organization. Fritjof Capra writes, "social institutions . . . exist for specific purposes. At the same time, organizations are communities of people who interact with one another . . ." (Capra, 2002, p. 125). This distinction helps us see the necessity of both formal and informal networks of interaction. The formal networks are generally designed, the informal are generally emergent. What we need to see, however, is that the informal networks are where new life and innovation arise, and the most resilient organizations have the dominant characteristics of living entities."

But secondly it helps us understand that we are dealing with two dimensions of ecclesial life. The first, the ordered ways of being together, of managing power and information flow, are predictable and fairly stable structures that are amenable to our control. The second, the informal and emergent structures of the living community, partake of the qualities of nonlinear systems, complex adaptive systems, and are the domain of Spirit. Living networks are fluid and fluctuating, and knowledge is often tacit and not articulated. The stronger these networks, the more the organization can learn and grow. Supporting the growth and strength of these networks is key to an organization's ability to thrive.

If the fall of Christendom and the shift from modernity to post-modernity are the two primary conditions of our time, together they generate the conditions that push us to consider the requirements of a leadership and learning community. We live in a time of wildly

---

"See the research of De Geus for the Shell Group, "The Living Company," The Harvard Business Review, 1997.

increasing complexity and the explosion of information. No single wise leader, nor even a small team, can master these conditions. Any organization which would thrive in this new world must learn to maximize its learning potential, cultivating knowledge and flexibility by becoming a *learning community*.

This requires a new kind of leadership, and a new relation between leaders and learners. During the predictable environment of the Industrial Revolution it was possible for one or two experts to analyze a situation and set direction from the top. In the complexity of our time this is no longer possible. We must find ways to harness the knowledge and goodwill of entire tribes of people in order to find our way forward. And we must decentralize decision-making power in order to maximize adaptability and the speed at which we can respond to a changing environment. *There is no way forward in the* missio Dei *apart from liberating the power of informal networks.* [12]

One of the studies of learning communities in Tasmania in the late 1990s described the leadership vision of a dynamic learning community like this: "leadership is a dynamic and collaborative *process* in which leadership roles are not defined . . . Leadership is therefore *created* as individuals and groups interact and collaborate." (Kilpatrick, Falk & Johns, 1998). In this view, developed in the midst of increasing complexity and rapid change, leadership is a *process* and something more like *an intervention* rather than the characteristic of one or two individuals. "The most powerful organizational learning and collective knowledge sharing grows through informal relationships and personal networks—via working conversations in communities of practice." (Capra, 2002, p. 108).

---

[12] This point is also strongly made in Steve Addison's recent work, *Movements That Change the World* (Smyrna, DE: Missional Press, 2009) 71ff.

In the language of Ephesians 4, "From him the whole body, joined and held together by every supporting ligament, grows and builds itself up in love, as each part does its work." It is the point of connection that is critical. We have to connect every part of the body in a healthy way to the other parts so that the gifts can function appropriately to bring maturity. This sounds suspiciously like the experience of Semco. What holds the centre together is shared purpose, and that requires an ongoing conversation. Mort Ryerson, chairman of Perot Systems, writes: ". . . we must realize that our task is to call people together often, so that everyone gains clarity about who we are, who we've just become, who we still want to be. If the organization can stay in a continuous conversation about who it is and who it is becoming, then leaders don't have to undertake the impossible task of trying to hold it all together." (Wheatley, 1997)

The leadership community thus creates a bridge between two worlds. One intention is to move away from traditional definitions of power to generate new kinds of partnerships, new leadership "spaces" and a culture of leadership, as opposed to the pyramidal structure where decisions flow down and trust and hope flow up – where learning is never maximized and the bulk of the people are passive.

If we are moving away from traditional definitions of power, what do we do with traditional language? As noted above, we create and maintain our worlds with language.[13] This constructivist insight points to

---

[13] I value the insight that organizations are heliotropic: they move toward the energy. Mark Lau Branson writes in *Memories, Hopes and Conversations* that, "we socially construct our world . . . and . . . we have the power to create what we imagine. It follows that a process for facilitating organizational change would consciously focus on empowering employees to believe they can make a difference; rewarding leaders who know how to empower others; and directing the energy of the system towards the positive, generative, and creative life forces . . ." (Rowman & Littlefield, 2004. p. 39)

the huge challenge we face as we attempt to recontextualize and redeem words that have been colonized by modernity and technocratic practices: words like *leadership, pastor, apostle, missional,* and *church*.

Some will argue that these words are beyond redemption. There are many who want to leave the language of "Christian" or "church" behind. Language and the way we use words changes, and it's necessary to *re-member* language. In the process of wrestling with these symbols and reconnecting them with meaning we become an interpretive community. In order to recover the best of our common heritage and move forward together we must communicate across boundaries, across *worlds of language*.

That task will be much easier if we remember the stories we share. To the extent that we are rooted in shared memory, we will find the task of listening together easier and more fruitful. Even in these times of tremendous fragmentation, we will have to hear the stories of Scripture as *our stories* in order to work together. Yet we have to listen with ears that are also tuned to our culture, because God is at work all around us, outside the walls. He is the God who says, "Behold, I do a *new thing.* "

The Five-Fold Ministry - *Then and Now*

A variety of scholars have pointed out that in the New Testament church a plurality of elders existed. Moreover, certain types of leaders appear to have held currency across churches, with a trans-local ministry. In a similar way we are seeing the rise of apostolic teams today.

Our language of "teams," like other language, is heard in the context of our experiences. A team is not the same as a community. In one environment, a team is formed to assist leaders to develop and implement their vision. In another environment a community is formed around a shared sense of passion and purpose (belonging). In the team environment success is understood as empowering the group to reach agreed goals. In the community environment success is understood as empowering individuals to belong and to reach their creative potential.

144

In the team environment roles tend to be set in concrete and leaders are indispensable. In the community environment leaders may be invisible, and leadership roles and functions are often shared. In his take on leadership as process Dwight Friesen observed that, "Leadership is about conversation. Leadership has less to do with the clarity of vision, and much more do to with the quality of conversation. How one fosters conversation is everything. Bringing self to the table, creating open space, speaking, naming, surrendering the need to be right, etc. Hidden agendas, unstated vision, passive aggressive needs to control, and rigid categories are just a few of the many ills ready to subvert [a learning] conversation." (Friesen, 2005).[14]

The language to describe these teams and their functioning varies according to received tradition and present context. But the roles that are appearing have familiar traits, and I am going to build on several sources here. To begin with I will restate: adaptive leadership is a function of context and *telos* – the end goal. Leadership, whether centralized or dispersed, is always sensitive to unique conditions, richly connected, and purposeful.

Furthermore, I want to note the need for creative tension in a strong leadership community.[15] This tension often comes up in anecdotal descriptions of creative engagement in new kingdom initiatives, but is not always clearly articulated. I understand it as the tension between the artists and engineers – those who are sensitive to emergence, and those who push for design. If we were to frame this theologically, we might reference Irenaeus, "the Word and the Spirit as the two hands of the Father in the world" (Against Heresies). We need

---

[14] Note also that German sociologist Niklas Luhmann describes human community as "a network of conversations."

[15] The types needed are examined in detail in a somewhat different frame by Alan Hirsch and Tim Catchim in *The Permanent Revolution*. My framing is somewhat different.

both artists and engineers in a leadership community, and if one type is dominant it's unlikely that the expression of renewal will be sustainable. At times of adaptive challenge, initiative will pass more to the emergent type leader. We'll elaborate on this in the following chapter.[16]

In *The Sky is Falling* Alan Roxburgh describes five leadership types, building from the five types of Ephesians 4. But he does not slavishly follow Paul's listing. Rather, he begins with the poet (Roxburgh, 2005, p. 164).

The poet helps people make sense of their experiences. The word in the prologue of John tells how Jesus "became flesh and lived among us" (Jn 1:14a). In a similar way, the poet shapes words so that what was hidden and invisible becomes known. Poets remove the veil and give language to what people are experiencing. This is only possible when the poet lives within the traditions and narratives of the people - "living reflexively in the traditions…The poet listens to the rhythms and meanings occurring beneath the surface" (Roxburgh, 2005, p. 164). But the poet also has a prophetic bent: poets immerse themselves in the stories running beneath the surface of the culture. Then they "critique their claims and pretensions on the basis of the memory and tradition of the community" (Roxburgh, 2005, p. 165).

The leadership of poets, however, is not expressed in a modern manner. Poets are less advice-givers and more image- and metaphor-framers. "What churches need are not more entrepreneurial leaders with wonderful plans for their congregation's life, but poets with the imagination and gifting to cultivate environments within which people might again understand how their traditional narratives apply to them today…" (Roxburgh, 2005, p. 166).

---

[16] In terms of complexity and emergence, Capra is helpful in his discussion of the need for creative tension in any learning process. "Since power is embodied in all social structures, the emergence of new structures will always challenge power relations" (Capra, 2002. p. 124).

Finally, "poets make available a future that does not exist as yet; they are *eschatologically* oriented. From this environment, a missional imagination emerges." (Roxburgh, 2005, p. 167). As we would expect, poets had little value in the churches of modernity during which we sought to define problems toward a solution. But poets don't bring solutions; rather they bring questions that invite dialogue. Poets do not accept the view of a congregation as a tool for impacting the world, but as the location of God's work of redemption and the incipient present-future of the kingdom.

In a study in Tasmania among innovative community groups, a new type of leader was described as a "boundary crosser." (Kilpatrick, Falk & Johns, 2002, p. 1). This type of person helped to generate connections between different groups working with a similar purpose. We might see this person as a "networker," however, they are networking with a purpose. They are both visionary and pastoral, something of a crossover between the pastor and prophetic type. These types are sometimes in formal leadership roles, but more often are a roving, informal type. This is really a new type, and does not correspond to the role we describe when we use the broad-brush label "pastor."

Roxburgh's second leadership type is the prophet. Prophets desire that the people of God rediscover the Word of God. "While poets invite dialogue in awareness and understanding, prophets call people to act on that knowledge." (Roxburgh, 2005, p. 168). These are the ones impatient with dialogue, and pushing for movement. He also notes that liminality is the rich soil of prophetic imagination. "It provides an environment where people are aware that they've lost their world and the connection with their most determinative stories." (Roxburgh, 2005, p. 169).

In liminal times prophets do not develop strategies for returning to the past, but rather they cultivate an environment that enables reengagement with God's story. In a time when the gospel has been reduced to morals and values or to spiritual experience, it is difficult to encounter the sovereign Lord of history. But the prophet creates situations that compel the community to re-inhabit its foundational stories. "The poet's primary concern is for the people and the desire to inspire in them new insight. The prophet's primary concern is giving tangible expression to what God is saying to the people." (Roxburgh, 2005, p. 171).

But there is another leadership type that is rising in the face of complex challenges. This type is of special interest, because it takes a unique combination of gifts to hold together the diverse leadership teams needed in these turbulent times. Likely this new type is a combination of apostolic, prophetic, and poetic. Lawrence Miller identifies them as *synergists.*

The Synergist

According to Miller, the synergist is the key to holding together diverse communities of leadership types. Miller describes a synergist as "... a leader who has escaped his or her own conditioned tendencies toward one style and incorporated, appreciated and unified each of the styles of leadership on the life-cycle curve." (Miller, 1990, p. 166).

The synergist guards this ethos; his role is to foster and maintain a creative and open space within the team so that no one role dominates. She helps maintain clarity of vision and the investment is in internal capital. As Mort Ryerson puts it, the primary task of being a leader is to make sure that the organization knows itself (Deering, Dilts, & Russell, 2003).

A healthy functioning leadership team may look different tomorrow than it does today. It exists as an expression of a growing set of relationships in a living network, in the way spouses regard their marriage itself as a third person -- a living and breathing soul that is created out of their living relationship.

One of the destructive legacies of the church in modernity was to impose universal theology and universal models. This pushed us away from location and specific engagement toward abstractions. Canadian church leaders imported the latest successful American model. American leaders in Seattle attempted to apply the latest winning model from Los Angeles. This was tantamount to importing palm trees from Hawaii and planting them in downtown Chicago with the confidence that they would thrive and grow. It was naïve at best and it was "bad faith" at worst – a reluctance to do the work necessary to discern the context and God's local purpose.

In systems language, adaptive solutions are always created within the unique context of the specific organization, and they cannot be transferred willy-nilly into a new context. Fritjof Capra writes that "what business leaders tend to do is . . . to replicate a new structure that has been successful without transferring the tacit knowledge and context of meaning from which the new structure emerged." (Capra, 2002, p. 119).

In other words, we must generate *local learning* in order to generate effective engagement. But this also returns us to the question of leadership, because as noted above, different kinds of leaders are needed to support adaptive structures.

But perhaps the synergist is not entirely new. Using older language, Alan Roxburgh calls the synergist an Abbot/Abbess. Some communities, like The Order of Mission (TOM), have modeled their structure on one of the strongest missional movements of the last 2,000 years: the Celts.

The Celts united *two* roles at the centre of the team: *bishop and abbot.* The bishop was the missional (apostolic) leader, the abbot the pastoral leader. These two shared equal authority, the bishop stewarding the outward life of the community, and the abbot its inward life. This is similar to the structure we imagined for FORGE hubs in

Canada, where every local hub would have both a hub leader and a hub pastor.[17]

But what makes such an old model so relevant and fresh today? In the Celtic communities in the fifth to ninth centuries, Abbots and Abbesses did not function as authoritative command and control personalities,[18] but rather they were people who best embodied the living ideals of the community. They were concerned more with cultivating healthy environments rather than shaping specific actions or developing programs. They were not managers, but spiritual elders. The leaders of tomorrow shape environments as opposed to creating groups. "When the environment is healthy, people will find connection on their own . . ." (Myers, 2003, p. 79).

How do we find such people? The Abbots and Abbesses are among us, although many of them are operating outside of the organized and inherited church system. They are people who understand process, they are ready mentors, and they are friends of time. Roxburgh reminds us that, "the new leadership we need to cultivate isn't primarily about more knowledge and content; it's about how you form learning communities that are apprenticed into new skills and habits..." (Roxburgh, 2010, p. 115)

---

[17] This old structure is also mirrored in the contemporary new monastic community of Northumbria, as documented in *Encounters on the Edge*, No. 29, published by the *Sheffield Center*, 2008. 28.

[18] This squares well with the best research being done on leadership in companies making a successful transition to postmodern reality. One of the best known, VISA, was founded on the network model by Dee Hock. Hock writes, "Purpose and principle, clearly understood and articulated . . . are the genetic code of any healthy organization. To the degree that you hold purpose and principle in common you can dispense with command and control...The organization will become . . . a creative . . . vital, living set of beliefs" (*Birth of the Chaordic Age*, p. 116).

Abbots and Abbesses and perhaps synergists -- have rich gifts of wisdom and walk with a deep sense of the living presence of Christ. They are natural fathers and mothers to those around them. Frequently they walk with a limp. They regard life as sacramental and they are lifelong learners. Community forms naturally around such people. Some have never occupied formal leadership roles, and many have been marginalized as disloyal critics because they do not accept the status quo and they ask uncomfortable questions.

When you focus on winning, you will lose.
When you focus on not losing, you will lose.
Pay attention to your inner balance.
Then perhaps you have a chance to win. (Pascale, Milleman, Gioja, 2000, p. 242).

In the first chapter I referenced Gareth Brandt. He noted that a new developmental stage has been created for young adults in Western culture. I argued that a new developmental stage has emerged for entire communities in transition. New experience grows out of new and unique cultural conditions. Moreover, new leadership types are also emerging in these unique conditions. I believe that the synergists (or abbots/abbesses) actually represent leaders who have hit the wall (stage four in the map in *The Critical Journey*). These ones dwelt for a while in liminal space, and then emerged into the next phase: the journey outward. As a result of surviving this transition they become ready guides for others in transition. They understand life on the margins, and have become comfortable in the experience of exile.

Conclusion

If leaders help us get to places we have never been, then leadership is largely an imaginative and poetic task. When we find ourselves off the map, we become open to new ways of being and doing.

We see in fresh ways. We learn to listen more deeply. The opportunity of liminal spaces is discovery, and also a renewal of community. We discover a fresh need for company when we are crossing an unknown sea.

Because the church is an organic reality, a changed environment means that new kinds of leadership will arise. This new leadership has new capacities, and looks different than the leadership we are familiar with. Naming these types is one way to begin wrestling with the new reality we are living in.[19]

We are traveling up the right side of the "U." As we go, we mark new signposts that help us to relocate ourselves. Organizations go through specific stages as they enter a new space. In the next chapter, we'll consider a framework for understanding organizational change, and then we'll consider in detail some of the new capacities adaptive leaders must possess to engage fruitfully in complex conditions.

The properties of liquid are emergent, and emergent properties produce emergent behavior. If our churches are in a phase transition, then we know two things:

they are not what they were, and not yet what they will become.

Instead of expending useless energy attempting to make a liquid into a solid,

instead of attempting to halt the transition and force a new stability, we have to learn to trust the God who delights to give us his kingdom.

We have to learn to wait.

---

[19] In a book just in print, Alan Hirsch describes the five types of Ephesians 4 as modes or intelligences. He argues that they are creation orders, and not limited to the church. This makes sense since Ephesians was written to a dynamic movement and not a settled, institutional culture. It's also easy to witness the reality of these modes in the marketplace! See Hirsch, *5iveQ: Re-Activating the Latent Intelligence and Capacities of the Body of Christ.* (100 Movements, 2017)

We are the people of the parenthesis –
at the end of one era and not quite at the beginning of another.
Maps no longer fit the new territory.
In order to make sense of it all,
we must cultivate a vision.

Jean Houston

Chapter 6

Imagining New Capacities

"[T]he key to dealing with a real crisis, one that goes beyond our personal realities, is in our abilities to move outside what we think of as normal. If the crisis is big enough, we have to reconsider the narrative or we can be destroyed by it" (Saul, 2014).

When our organizations are in crisis mode, it's only a matter of time before we arrive there with them. That's the way complex systems work: they are interdependent. Leaders, like the organizations they lead, find themselves caught in between the old world and the new. The maps we are using no longer describe the territory, compromising our ability to find the way forward.

In order to make new maps, we have to use language. Language both empowers and constrains. At best metaphors are lenses that enable us to see what is really going on. They allow an imaginative grasp that can transcend our rational analysis. Moreover, metaphors are a good filter; the, can increase contrast, depth and focus. Likewise words are tools for sense-making.

If this all seems esoteric, consider for a moment that language is the primary and indispensable vehicle for leadership. No individual or team can provide leadership without communicating. By our words we open or close possibilities, we open or close doors to new worlds. By his words God created the universe, and by his words he continues to uphold it.

This is also a good place to be reminded that leadership, like the church itself, must be transformed. Leadership must submit to the Spirit. The heart of Christian leadership is spiritual and Trinitarian. The church on mission is sustained by the Word and the Spirit, and expresses the heart of the Father and his desire to heal all things. Leadership functions best when it is non-hierarchical and communal, echoing the sustaining intimacy and eternal love and friendship that exists in the heart of the triune God.

There are several key implications of this. One is that leadership and transformation have a non-human, providential dimension. In the language of leadership we express ourselves with reference to vocation and gifting. Our priestly call, as with our gifts, is given by the Spirit. The church is sent for a purpose, to participate in God's mission of restoring all things. But if God is the one who sovereignly distributes, then we must function within the gifts God gives. Leaders can't simply choose a style, a new way of being as leaders; we are limited by our gifts and competencies and personality types. Leaders who are natural managers and administrators will not function well in the chaos of complex adaptive challenges. David could not wear Saul's armour. There is a lot we have to leave behind. Wendell Berry writes,

> To know what may be had by loss of having,
> To see what loss of time will make of seed
> In earth or womb, dark come to light, the saving
> Of what was lost in what will come –repaid
> In the visible pattern that will mark
> Whatever of the passing light is made (Berry, 1998, p. 20).

Most leaders in our day have some grief work to do; the longer we have been in leadership, the more likely this is the case. We can't move forward without having done that work, or our emotional attachment to the past will sabotage our future. The first half of this book was an attempt to ensure that the reader has begun that journey. But having embarked, with whatever baggage was necessary, we face a host of new questions. In this chapter we begin to mark signposts for an unknown future.

The task of leadership is changing, and changing substantially. The world we are entering is so new that many established leaders will not make the transition. Leaders raised in the new world, the digital, connected and visual world, have already adapted. But even they can't escape the reality of our exilic conditions. They must still be people on pilgrimage, even if the journey looks different for those born in liminality, just as it looked different for those born in the desert and not in Egypt. Joshua learned different capacities than did Moses.

The context of leadership has changed for at least the following reasons:

1. we are more relational and connected than ever, at the same time as we are more fragmented (participating in multiple worlds simultaneously);
2. we have moved from the centre to the margins, a religious marketplace where Christianity is just one option among many;
3. our mission (purpose) is shifting away from the insulated church (attractional and inward) to the parish and to the common good (incarnational and outward);
4. our mission is shifting from an individual pursuit to communal – the church as a body, a new political reality in the world;
5. the centre of authority has shifted from knowledge to relationship;
6. this shift in knowledge base combined with networked reality means that people *expect* to participate; and
7. complex conditions require us to leverage the intelligence and efforts of all God's people.

For these reasons and more, we need new leadership types. Next, we'll consider a framework for understanding leadership in context: a three-zone model for understanding organizations in transition. Viewing these dynamics, we'll be better able to understand the need for a new kind of leadership. Then we'll consider the particular competencies of these new leaders, competencies tied to their context and the requirements of adaptive challenge.

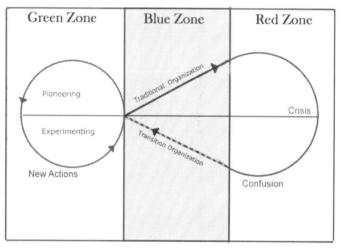

Figure 7. Organizational Culture Zones
Understanding Organizational Culture

In *The Missional Leader*, the authors identify three zones of organizational culture that churches and para-churches form: 1) the green zone, where complex (emergent) leadership is active; 2) the blue zone where managerial (traditional) leadership is active; and 3) the red or reactive zone. (Roxburgh & Romanuck, 2006, p. 40). Each zone, they note, has its unique leadership habits, skills, behaviours and imagination. The authors argue that apostolic leaders need to be equipped to help churches and para-churches understand the predominant zone in which they, as corporate entities, operate. Once we know ourselves we can then respond and adapt more readily to the changing context in order to engage effectively.

Identifying the zone of our organizational culture offers the possibility of bringing leaders across organizations into deep and broad-based, collaborative conversations — learning conversations — to help them cross-pollinate and devise approaches to navigating change that are both healthy and progressive.

According to Roxburgh and Romanuk, churches and organizations operating in the green zone, the *emergent* zone, are strongly adaptive. This means they tend to: 1. cultivate innovative experiments; 2. respond to context on the basis of their self-initiated (swarm and non-linear) interaction rather than waiting on a top-down, preplanned strategy; and 3. develop needed practices and structures for ongoing fruitful engagement with their context.[20]

Organizations tend to start out on the left side, in the emergent zone, initiated by creative, innovative types who are risk takers, responding to actual conditions. Over time, and with growth, however, organizations become mired in ways and means, and bureaucracy expands. The focus shifts from mission to maintenance.

Once the organization is well-established, risk-taking behaviours and emergent type leaders are moved to the margins. Often impatient with meetings and managers, these leader types move on to other experiments in creative organizations. This further reinforces the managerial culture at the core, and the organization moves into the blue zone, the *management* zone. In the management zone, churches and organizations no longer focus on adaptive skills but on passing on learned skills to the next generation of leaders. In this zone, organizational culture focuses on: 1. cultivating well-developed

---

[20] In every organization there will be both designed and emergent structures, and so there will always be both managerial and emergent behaviors. But when adaptive responses are needed the complex and emergent behaviors should prevail.

structures and programs; 2. practicing centralized planning; and 3. defining and implementing effectiveness measures.

Eventually the organization loses touch with its founding mission and becomes increasingly inward and protective of the status quo. It becomes ripe to be overtaken by competition, or upset by changing conditions. When threats arise, the organization works harder and not smarter. If the threat (and anxiety) increases, the organization moves into the red zone, the *reactive* zone. This shift can also be the result of the effort of key leaders to destabilize the organization in the face of an adaptive challenge. Whatever the cause, the priority becomes averting a crisis and returning the organization to a state of stability by using: 1. regulation; 2. measures that align the organization with its strategic objectives; and 3. bold, visionary plans designed to rouse the troops.

In order to survive into the future, all organizations must understand the preferred zone out of which they operate. Furthermore, they must evaluate the suitability of their mode of operation in light of the changes happening in their context; and they must be willing to make radical adaptations when necessary.

The authors make several key points in surveying the landscape. First, they note that a high percentage of churches and para-church organizations still operate out of a blue (middle) zone mentality, since this proved to be so effective in the once predictable environment. Secondly, over the past twenty years, as cultural change shifted into high gear, into the category of discontinuous (unpredictable) change, many leaders tightened the managerial belt, moving into the reactive zone, thereby decreasing their ability to respond to the new conditions.

Third, many younger leaders adopted an emergent zone response and have been learning critical adaptive skills needed for navigating the turbulent waters, skills that are desperately needed by managerial and reactive zone leaders. (Note that while emergent zone leadership is most needed now, this does not eliminate all traditional managerial behaviors.}

Finally, because of Western culture's pluralism, fragmentation, and increasing exposure to discontinuous change, leaders in all zones need to equip their communities in order to re-enter the biblical narrative. This will assist in fostering a fresh imagination for their unique context.

The Role of Leaders in Emergent Conditions

"I skate to where the puck is going to be, not to where it has been."[21]

The conditions of our time are unique and complex, and thus our need for leadership is likewise unique and complex. In the discussion that follows I use several different adjectives to describe leadership in complex conditions, including "adaptive," "complex" and "emergent." They mean the same thing.

Plowman *et al* researched the way leadership functions in complex conditions and found the following three mechanisms used by leaders in emergent, self-organizing systems: 1. leaders disrupt existing patterns, 2. they encourage novelty, and 3. they act as sense-makers (Plowman, Solansky, Beck, Baker, Kulkarni & Travis, 2007, p. 341-356).

---

[21] Attributed to Wayne Gretzky.

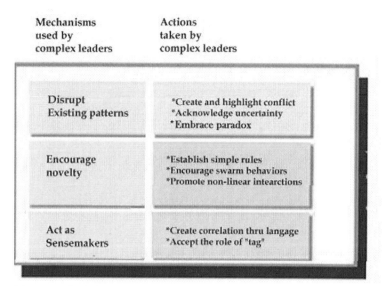

Figure 8. The Role of Leaders. Plowman et al. 2007.

When conditions have changed but an organization has not made any adaptive response, leaders play a role in pushing the system toward chaos by disrupting existing processes or patterns of behaviour. In the above frame, this means moving the organization into the red zone.

The authors describe two important actions by complex (emergent) leaders to disrupt existing patterns. First, they create and highlight conflict, emphasizing uncertainty, which traditional or performative leaders seek to increase stability and eliminate uncertainty.

When our structures and knowledge no longer match external conditions, it's time to talk! Busy leaders at the core of organizations are often the last to know that there is a disconnect. Once aware, their task is to highlight the problem, even in the face of disagreement or conflict. Inevitably, those who are conflict-averse will try to restore peace, perhaps denying there is a problem (I'm not lost, just disoriented!) The role of leaders is to continue to disrupt the system, highlight the changed conditions, and turn up the heat. These efforts enable

162

emergent self-organization, breaking down traditional boundaries and disrupting role definitions that have become set in cement.[22] Emphasizing uncertainty – the unknown future -- can generate openness to new learning and new listening and enable those who are willing to cross traditional boundaries, thus generating further instability.

The difference between emergent or complex leaders and traditional leaders is notable relative to risk-taking and innovation: Traditional leaders lead through command and control. They believe that vision and direction need to be communicated from the top down. Complex leaders prefer collaboration and networking. They encourage innovation by establishing simple rules and acting as enablers of emergent self-organization. Plowman *et al.* describe it as a paradoxical leadership approach: "On the one hand, the leaders tried to do what they thought 'good' leaders would do – articulate a vision and get others to buy into it. On the other hand, with something of a *laissez faire* attitude, they encouraged church members who had an interest in a particular program or ministry to get together with others sharing that interest and to try it." (Plowman, Solansky, Beck, Baker, Kulkarni & Travis, 2007, p. 350)

Creativity and imagination are closely linked to the work of the Spirit, and a lack of creativity may indicate a lack of dependence on God, or an overconfidence in one's own abilities. This calls for the exercise of our neglected imaginations, because imagination enables us to see alternatives – a much-needed skill in the complex, globalized world. Godly imagination enables a leader to tell an alternative story, seeing an alternate future in the places where the Spirit is working.

---

[22] There *will* be conflict, because power is embodied in social structures, and the emergence of new structures changes the power relations.

Plowman *et al* observe three phenomena at work in encouraging innovation. The first is the establishment of a few simple rules. Complex leaders are clear about the core issues, but ambiguous in terms of how to achieve them. The authors conclude: "What we saw was a tenacious rigidity about the principle, and complete flexibility about how to go about carrying out the principle." (Plowman, Solansky, Beck, Baker, Kulkarni & Travis, 2007, p. 350). This is typical of young organizations, where ways and means are not yet set in concrete.

The second is the 'swarm behaviour' of membership and staff. This refers to the swarm intelligence described earlier in social insects such as bees and ants. Similar behaviour is observable in organizations, when complex collective behaviour emerges from individuals who follow simple rules. "Termites construct their beautifully intricate colonial dwellings through processes that look anything but organized. Yet, out of the activities of termite construction gangs, that form and disperse in apparently disorganized patterns, there emerge coherently structured pillared halls and passageways, complete with air conditioning, that accommodate thousands of inhabitants." (Goodwin, 1999, p. 42)

At Metro Church, we always began the day with a breakfast, because many of our members had spent the night on the street. An elderly woman initiated the event, and soon others had gathered around her. It began with pancakes, then quickly evolved to gourmet sandwiches. Then one day a chiropractor set up his treatment table in one corner. Our simple rule, *let's find ways to serve the needs of our community*, has led to innovation and a complex ministry that involved food and health services. Eventually a social worker also set up a work space. Creative authority does not focus on the individual, but on the faith community and their collective participation and ownership of the call to service.

The final element in encouraging innovation is the promotion of connections between people, and in particular, non-linear interactions and emotional connections. Compare this to Paul in Ephesians 4:15-16: – ". . . speaking the truth in love, we will in all things grow up into him who is the head, that is, Christ. From him the whole body, joined and held together by every supporting ligament, grows and builds itself up in love, as each part does its work." This very organic image describes something powerful that happens at the point of connection. Non-linear connections describe relationships that are non-hierarchical, and from a systemic viewpoint, somewhat random. Connections may not be driven by organizational goals; instead they reach across traditional working boundaries.

These rich interactions can lead to unexpected outcomes. Complex systems are relationally driven, and this approach to leadership is essential for the emergence of novelty and creativity. At Metro we did not use the pulpit to dispense decisions about what is to be done. Rather, we remind people of our purpose, and then challenge them to respond as they see fit. We often gather a diverse group of people to brainstorm new ideas. A few simple rules and random connections can lead to complex patterns of collective action.

Experimenting into the Future

Many people believe that we must know how to do something before we do it. As we saw earlier with Richard Branson, if this were literally true, many great innovations would never have occurred. Moreover, where cause and effect used to be clear and observable, we now understand that complex systems are neither knowable nor predictable. One of the ways we describe this complexity is by the phrase "sensitive initial conditions."

Meteorologists used to believe that the prediction of weather patterns depended on the quality of the model of the atmospheric processes involved and on the level of detail of the data. However, it turns out that the system is so complex that neither of those will allow accurate long-term predictions of the weather. The butterfly effect describes sensitivity to initial conditions. The butterfly flapping its wings in the Amazon may impact the path of a jetliner in Asia or cause a typhoon in Indonesia. (Goodwin, 1999, p. 43). Researchers have discovered that very small initial differences can lead to highly divergent conditions, such as whether or not a typhoon will develop. As far as weather forecasting is concerned, any small error in specifying initial conditions, even the rounding errors that accompany computation, will grow exponentially. Errors will then rapidly overwhelm the calculation, and computed states will diverge from real states to the point that the prediction fails.

It appears that this sensitivity to initial conditions, or closely related dynamic properties, may govern a great variety of processes that we now regard as complex. The physiological activities of our bodies and brains, ecological and evolutionary processes, and economies all seem to be characterized by mixtures of order and chaos, such that precise predictions become impossible. Scientific knowledge, originally seen to make possible the prediction and manipulation of nature, appears now to be pointing us toward a new relationship with the natural world based on sensitive observation and *participation*, rather than control.[23] (We'll return to this theme later.)

On the one hand, this places us in an unimagined world, strange and unpredictable. On the other hand, it lets us release the illusion of control, which frees us to participate in new ways in the unfolding future. Rather than having a clear map that enables us to find the future, an alternative view is that the creative process is a dynamic learning process, and the best we can possibly have at the outset is a vision of where we want to be and a hypothesis about how to get there. Then we 'create and adjust.' We learn how to do something truly new by doing it. Or as Native Americans have said it, we make the path by walking.

---

[23] "Participation" names one of the unique features of the Gospel. The intimacy Jesus offers is participation in the inner life of God. John 15:5, John 17.

What Senge *et al* describe as *presencing* is the experience of the coming in of the new and the transformation of the old. Once a group crosses this threshold, nothing remains the same. Individuals connect with both mind and heart. Remember Bagger Vance? "The wisdom in your hands is greater than the wisdom of your head will ever be." Members and the group as a whole begin to operate with a heightened level of energy and sense of future possibility.

Maybe it's not quite that simple, but almost. The way the future is birthed is not like it used to be. We used to measure, then plan, then implement. Not anymore. The speed of change and the interconnectivity of the world have changed all that. Now what we do is create prototypes.

Prototyping demands that first you let go, you empty out all the stuff you thought you needed. Then you determine what you really need and provide prototype solutions for those real needs in real time. You observe and adapt based on what happens next. You enter the feedback loop, and dance between inspiration and experiment. A prototype is simply exploring by doing, creating a little landing strip of the future that allows for hands-on testing.

Metro began as an experiment among youth who were looking for a way to reach out to the street community and the urban poor. It quickly moved from an evening event at the gospel mission to a morning event at a dance venue. As the experiment gained traction, it became a breakfast, a clothing exchange, and a church meeting. Then it morphed into a whole-person spiritual/health program that mixed middle-class "normies" with all kinds of people in addictions and recovery. We saw dramatic encounters as light broke into the darkness of the street.

Prototyping is at the heart of every creative design process. A prototype models our current best understanding of the process or goal to enable an iterative adaptation to a new environment. We act before we've figured everything out, because we can't know all we need to know in advance when the situation is truly new and unique. We have to begin before we are ready.

Jacques Derrida, the continental philosopher, writes on *l'avenir*, to come. He recognizes that what is predictable is not the future, but only our past projected forward. Derrida, considered agnostic by most commentators, often evidences a profound faith in a God he refuses to name. Comfortable in the ambiguity of not knowing, he stands and waits for the future to arrive.

In general, I try to distinguish between what one calls the future and *l'avenir*. The future is that which- tomorrow, later, next century - will be. There's a future which is predictable, programmed, scheduled, foreseeable. But there is a future, *l'avenir* (to come) which refers to someone who comes whose arrival is totally unexpected. For me, that is the real future. That which is totally unpredictable. The other who comes without my being able to anticipate their arrival. So if there is a real future beyond this other known future, it's *l'avenir* in that it's the coming of the other when I am completely unable to foresee their arrival. (White & Derrida, 2007)

In January 1999, Peter Senge met with a group in Cambridge, Massachusetts, who were attempting to strategically address some large and persistent environmental issues related to manufacturing. A highlight of the meeting was when John Elter told a story from his days at Xerox that resulted in Xerox's first fully digital generation of copiers. A group of engineers, normally walled in by their respective silos, had asked the question, "If nature creates no waste, shouldn't we do the same?" Elter's team pioneered design innovations that resulted in a product with only about two hundred parts (versus 2,000 for its predecessor), all of which went together with clips and screws for disassembly, ninety-two per cent of which could be remanufactured and ninety-six per cent recycled (Senge, Scharmer, Jaworski, & Flowers, 2005, p. 152).

Acting before we are ready puts us in a completely different space, where it is possible to shape our actions by the unknown field of the future rather than by the patterns of the past, trusting that the Spirit will lead us into God's preferred future. The "church art" of listening to the whole and creating space for the new is leadership at its best (Morse, 2012, p. 149).

If the future is unknown, then we are in a liminal space. We are not what we were, and not yet what we will be, caught between the existing world and what's next. That's why innovative leaders have an unusual ability: they know how to embrace paradox. TS Eliot describes the field of the future and nature of paradoxical movement.

> *In order to arrive at what you do not know*
> *You must go by a way which is the way of ignorance.*
> *In order to possess what you do not possess*
> *You must go by the way of dispossession.*
> *In order to arrive at what you are not*
> *You must go through the way in which you are not.*
> *And what you do not know is the only thing you know*
> *And what you own is what you do not own*
> *And where you are is where you are not.* (Eliot, 1960)

Bill Buker argues that there are three orders of change. (Buker, 2003, p. 148). First-order change can be understood as common sense. Something isn't working, so we try something different. Habits are hard to break, however, so the new behaviour may not last long. Second-order change usually involves a crisis and hitting a wall. When alcoholics suddenly realize their life is out of control, they admit they are powerless. This opens them up to a new narrative and a new relationship to the problem. But it's a paradoxical location: powerlessness opens the possibility of surrender. Note: surrender exists here in potential only. Many addicts are still trying to manipulate the system at this stage. Surrender is the third order of change.

Buker describes the shift through the second and third orders of change as epistemological. The addict suddenly knows herself and the system in a fresh way. There is a fresh perspective, a new relationship to herself and to the problem. In some ways, the addict now stands outside the system. Surrender is a paradoxical and liminal posture, and one required of those who enter the kingdom (Matt 19:23-30).

Remember our climbers at the opening of chapter 4? There were a number of elements of paradox in the story. First, they had to go down to go up. Acclimatization to high altitudes required this adaptive behavior. Second, the ones who survived were constantly reflecting not just on the conditions of the climb, but on their relationship to alpine climbing and on their own motivations for the climb. The ones who were eventually successful, like Gerlinde Kaltenbrunner, were philosophical: living in a place of surrender, in which they are both personally invested, yet detached from the idea of success. In reality, they are detached from the image of themselves as successful. They use the language of surrender, even though most do not talk about a Higher Power.

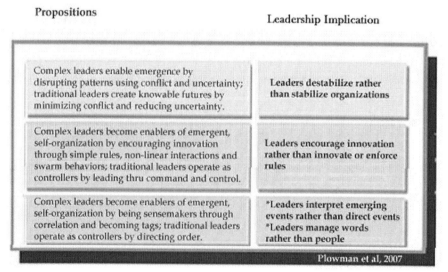

Figure 9. Traditional vs Complex Leaders. Plowman et al.

Sensemaking

1. Complex leaders disrupt existing patterns, encourage innovation, and they act as sense-makers. Sense-making is the process by which individuals "construct meaningful explanations for situations and their experiences within those situations" (Plowman, Solansky, Beck, Baker, Kulkarni & Travis, 2007, p. 351). One role of leaders in a complex organization is to tell a new story, to change the perception of a situation. This is a poetic leadership function. The poet helps us make sense of our experience. The words in the prologue of John tell how Jesus "became flesh and lived among us." In a similar way, the poet shapes words so that what was hidden and invisible becomes known. Poets remove the veil and give language to what people are experiencing. This is only possible when the poet lives within the traditions and narratives of the people, "living reflexively in the traditions…The poet listens to the rhythms and meanings occurring beneath the surface" (Roxburgh, 2005, p. 164).

What this means is that leaders interpret change rather than create it. They are map-makers and meaning-makers. Leaders as sense-makers are critical when our traditions and frameworks for understanding reality are crumbling. Leaders must be able to scan the environment and interpret issues that might influence decision-making and strategic direction. Moreover, the congregation itself must become an interpretive community, doing theology locally, as noted above, and doing it together. This involves reflecting actively on the changing local conditions, and gathering to share stories.[24] It means making new

---

[24] "Leadership involves the creation of powerful narratives," one scholar has said. "The skilled leader is one who can both articulate and embody a complex of

connections and trying new things, assimilating complex ideas and trying on new frameworks for organizing what is heard, seen, and discovered.

Sense-making as a task is related to *discernment,* a core practice for churches in renewal. Ruth Haley Barton defines discernment as "an ever-increasing capacity to 'see' or discern the work of God in the midst of the human situation so that we can align ourselves with the work God is doing" (Barton, 2012, p. 20). Moreover, discernment is a *communal* process. Barton lists five foundational beliefs related to discernment.

1. Spiritual discernment, by definition, takes place in and through the Trinity.
2. The impulse to discern—to want to respond to the leading of Spirit – is itself a good spirit that needs to be cultivated.
3. It requires a deep belief – *confidence* – in the goodness of God.
4. It grows from a conviction that love is our ultimate calling.
5. It requires a commitment to doing the will of God as it is revealed to us – surrender.

Discernment is a quality of attentiveness to God that develops over time as an ability to sense God's heart and purpose. It requires us to "test the spirits," and is a spiritual practice that, as with all spiritual practices, opens us to the activity of God beyond what we can do for ourselves (Barton, 2012, p. 57, 62). This means asking good questions: questions which create space for a new imagination. And it means cultivating solitude as space for listening. The more this task is understood as a communal responsibility, the more likely that an adaptive response will be made.

---

stories." Joel Kurtzman, "An Interview with Howard Gardner," *Strategy and Business* (First Quarter 1999): 2

Remember Otto Scharmer standing in front of his burning home in chapter 3? His gaze went from the problem, the fire and the imminent loss, to a place of inner knowledge. He moved from seeing the immediate details to accessing his inner self, and in that quiet place of presence he discovered inner freedom. This sort of knowledge is an invitation to move beyond ourselves toward our life's purpose. The task is really to become superb listeners.

Leaders tend to become activists, people who "get something done." However, in times of transition, leaders will encounter ever-increasing demands that they set direction and offer answers. But this is precisely what we must not do, because it compromises an adaptive response. How will we find the courage to withstand the anxious demands of people moving into unfamiliar territory? We must cultivate the inner life, and in particular, cultivate solitude as space for listening.

In the West, we have tended to see silence and solitude as vehicles for escape, as a selfish response rather than as a means to encounter the world afresh. But silence and solitude are not escapist; rather, they allow us to find ourselves and God in fresh ways. They allow us to find the peaceful centre without which we will soon burn out, or become tyrants seeking our value in our actions. Silence and solitude open space for hospitable space where we can listen more deeply. Len Sweet writes that leaders "must listen when they can so they may act when they must." (Sweet, 2004, p. 60). Henri Nouwen offers that,

To listen is very hard, because it asks of us so much interior stability that we no longer need to prove ourselves by speeches, arguments, statements, or declarations. True listeners no longer have an inner need to make their presence known. They are free to receive, to welcome, to accept... Listening is a form of spiritual hospitality by which you invite strangers to become friends, to get to know their inner selves more fully, and even to dare to be silent with you (Nouwen, 1996).

It is in solitude that we will find the words that make sense; they will grow out of a rich inner life. Jesus even promised that they will bubble up in us like water from a spring (Jn 7.38; 16:13).

According to Plowman *et al*, sense-making involves two special activities: first, assuming the role of a 'tag', and secondly, creating correlation through language. The role of a 'tag' boils down to the ability to focus attention on core issues; that is, leaders give meaning to emergent events by reframing them. (Plowman, Solansky, Beck, Baker, Kulkarni & Travis, 2007, p. 350). Tags, similar to the function of a tag in Facebook or on Twitter, direct attention to what is important. They help to empower particular behaviors in relation to the emerging need.

Complex leaders become enablers of self-organization by being sense-makers through correlation, which they do through language. "Leaders manage words rather than manage people." (Plowman, Solansky, Beck, Baker, Kulkarni & Travis, 2007, p. 347). In emerging systems leaders use language to help give meaning to unfolding events; they *interpret* events rather than direct them. Plowman *et al.* found that with language as a medium, leaders can "establish the identity of the objects, events, and actors that constitute their social environment" (Plowman, Solansky, Beck, Baker, Kulkarni & Travis, 2007, p. 352). This is critical as organizations move out of their comfort zones because ill-chosen language can constrain rather than open space, if we are unable to articulate what is new, or if our only language for leadership evokes hierarchy and control.

Perhaps one meaning of speaking with new tongues is finding a new language to describe what is surprising and fresh (Acts 2.4). By using a consistent language, leaders give meaning to the changes that are underway. We need a new language for leadership, just as we need a new imagination for the church.

But lest we take this new information and drop it onto the old map, let's talk about another component of biblical practice. Community has often been an aerosol word in Western churches: the practice has been incredibly thin. Networked reality and the nature of adaptive challenge are pushing us to rediscover its operation; indeed *participation* may be the watchword as we seek a new future together.

Recovering Biblical Imagination:
Participation, Conversation and the Trinity

Participation is at the heart of ecclesiology, because it represents a deep truth about who God is. "Mission is ... not the saving of disembodied souls *out of* creation but participation with God in the redeeming of whole persons to become fully alive *in* creation." (Hastings, 2012). We participate in God's life. Van Gelder and Zscheile write, "A participatory understanding opens up a highly reciprocal view of the God-world-church relationships, in which the church shares in the Triune God's own vulnerable engagement with the world . . . Imitation tends to stress what God *has done.* Participation invites us into what God *is doing* and *will continue to do* as God's promises in Christ are brought to fulfillment" (Gelder & Zscheile, 2011, pp. 109-111).

I opened this chapter with some notes on language as the primary vehicle of leadership. Recall Dwight Friesen's observation: "Leadership is about conversation. Leadership has less to do with the clarity of vision, and much more do to with the quality of conversation" (Friesen, 2005, p.80). Postmoderns may admit that hierarchy grants the illusion of structural efficiency, but they recognize that the model is from the corporate and technological world. In the biological world, life loves redundancy. *Why not* have fifty pastors in a community of two hundred adults? Peter Senge offers this definition of leadership: "Leadership is the capacity of the community to bring forth new realities" (Senge, 1990). This definition calls us to a level of shared leadership that evokes a developmental model -- something closer to a family than a corporate structure. As we participate in the life of the Trinity, God's work in caring for the world is expressed through us. Paul Stevens notes the importance of coinherence of the Trinity for every member-ministry of the whole people of God: "The Father creates, providentially sustains, and forms a covenantal framework for all existence. The Son incarnates, mediates, transfigures and redeems. The Spirit empowers and fills with God's own presence. But each shares in the other—coinheres, interpenetrates, cooperates—so that it is theologically inappropriate to stereotype the ministry of any one" (Stevens, 1999, p. 57).

Some practitioners are building on the concept of team leadership to look for more open models. Some like the metaphor of air traffic controller (ATC). An ATC doesn't fly the airplane, he only establishes safe paths for flight and coordinates their interaction once airborne. The ATC is almost an invisible part of the process, but his or her role is essential in enabling the flight. Others, like Isaac Stern, prefer the metaphor of a symphony conductor.

A good conductor does not merely tell everyone what to do; rather he helps everyone to hear what is so. For this he is not primarily a telling but a listening individual: even while the orchestra is performing loudly he is listening inwardly to silent music. He is not so much commanding as he is obedient.

"The conductor conducts by being conducted. He first hears, feels, loses himself in the silent music; then when he knows what it is he finds a way to help others hear it too. He knows that music is not made people playing instruments, but rather by music playing people" (Stern & Potok, 2001 p. 55).

Many new communities eschew titles and labels, recognizing that labels can separate people in the community from one another. Story after story from the corporate world relates how the executive leader in a struggling company eschewed her title, opened her office door, and became available to everyone. This change in ethos stimulated dialogue and learning, and generated new levels of ownership. When combined with an open space where it was okay for everyone regardless of pay-scale to challenge accepted wisdom, learning and effectiveness were accelerated. This was VISA's story, and also Pixar's.

Labeling a person by one's function (for example, "pastor") not only creates distance, but may damage the wholeness of the relationship and limit our biblical imagination, such as the recognition that others function as pastors and leaders in their workplace or in other communities. The point is that it's the BODY – the collective – that is primary and not the individual member, however gifted that person might appear (our need to honor 'the weaker member.'). We need the collective wisdom of the whole in order to engage in complex conditions.

Remember the story of Semco: it went from a traditional business to a free-for-all corporation, with as little centralized control as possible. Semco employees set their own salaries and working hours, and decided for themselves how and when they would produce new products. Semco's best businesses were ones that employees invented themselves in response to some opportunity they saw at the ground level. As a result, Semco looked increasingly less like a business organization and more like an immune system. Its knowledge was everywhere; control was radically decentralized; its reaction time to a changed environment was profoundly quick.

By spreading power around instead of hoarding it, Semler was practicing the lesson of *The Starfish and the Spider*. Cut the head off a spider and it dies. Cut a leg off a starfish, which has no head, and it grows a new one. Some of the major principles of decentralization include:

1. When attacked, a decentralized organization tends to become even more open and decentralized.
2. An open system doesn't have central intelligence; the intelligence is spread throughout the system.
3. Open systems can easily mutate.
4. Put people into an open system and they'll automatically want to contribute.

5. When attacked, centralized organizations tend to become even more centralized (Brafman & Beckstrom, 2006).

Consider that the church is actually a radically-decentralized organization. It has only one head, but that head is the Spirit (our nerve system for guidance and decision-making) distributed fully in every member. This has made the church both adaptable and very difficult to stop. As a complex system, it is independent and does not refer decisions up and down a theoretical chain of command. When left to function autonomously and locally, it has mutated and adapted to every culture through history. The church has only become centralized and rigidly structured when we have forced it into a narrow cultural mold and emphasized the importance of human leaders and authority structures. This "franchise" mentality made some sense in the West in modernity, but now it is demonstrating its fragility. Worse, this cloning activity has sapped some of our knowledge of how the body should function in unique conditions.

Drive down any major city route and you will find a McDonald's or Burger King or Tim Horton's. These franchises are a tribute to modern concepts of control and scale. No matter what franchise you enter, you will find the same menu with the same items at the same prices. There is comfort in this, and franchises have had great success for this reason. But times are changing!

Parallel to this reality, there are a growing number of people celebrating unique and limited beers, brewed on site and often with locally-sourced ingredients. Each microbrewery takes on its own identity, even though they share common aspects of architecture and design. These businesses represent 'local flavour' and our culture's shift towards the local and unique and away from the controlled and universal.

In the past, it was a comfort for an increasingly transient and mobile society to be able to travel nation-wide and find a familiar franchise of church. No matter where you went, you could find a United Methodist Church or a First Baptist Church. You would be sure to find a fairly universal experience of liturgy and theology. Denominational loyalty was prized over local initiative, and people sought out the local franchise as they moved from place to place. It was an *advantage* in those years to maintain the local franchise.

Participation

However, that was then and this is now! That was before the digital revolution that heightened our ability to customize, personalize, individualize. Moreover, there has been a backlash against the franchise mentality as stale and boring. As a result, emerging generations are less connected to the franchise worldview. Denominations have weakened overall, and those that are adapting are developing a greater diversity of expression. People are looking for a church expression that is unique and unrepeatable. This cultural shift has some profound implications, not the least of which is an invitation to explore what unique shape and local flavor a particular expression of the church might develop as it relates to its context in a way that gives life.

In biology, a franchise is a *monoculture*. Monocultures are stable, easy to rationalize, and very vulnerable. A single virus can wipe out an entire generation of innovation. The gradual extinction of the homogeneous church will also mean a recovery of parish: the church can play a role in gathering all the people in a particular place as stakeholders in the expanding local story of *shalom*, reconciling people across their tribal differences. And by giving local people a voice, the flavour of the church and its *ownership* are going back to the people. Peter Block draws out some implications. "The shift is to believe that the task of leadership is to provide context and produce engagement, to tend to our social fabric. It is to see the leader as one whose function is to engage groups of people in a way that creates accountability and commitment . . ." (Block, 2009, p. 88)

179

When the local Body of Christ is trusted and empowered, and not forced to conform to one particular model, it will have demonstrated an ability to engage creatively and thrive in a wide diversity of contexts. Each new incarnation can be unique: the DWCC in Windsor, the Story in Sarnia, the Urban Abbey in Thunder Bay, the Vineyard in Winnipeg, Grandview Calvary in Vancouver. As we shift from being consumers to producers, we do two things simultaneously: 1. We leverage the knowledge and creativity of every member; and 2. We engage people in the area of their passion. The implications are seen in stories like that of Pixar and Semco, but also in that of Eric von Hippel and the mountain bike.

When users step into active engagement and become *participants*, innovation moves to the edge of the network from the heavily-strategic centre. At the centre, movement is slow, committee-oriented, and overly risk-averse. At the edges it is creative, risk-engaging, and fast.

As told in the book *Democratizing Innovation*, a few trail-rising gearheads intent on customizing their biking experience began building more suitable bikes by swapping tips, parts, and experiences as they went. They accelerated the creation of a new sport which we now know as mountain-biking. (Hippel, 2005). We tend to think that the centre defines things, when in reality, it's the edges that are critical to life. As the authors of *Surfing the Edge of Chaos* note, "'As long as one operates in the middle of things,' states science writer William Thompson, 'one can never really know the nature in which one moves.' The visual cortex of our brain directs our eyes to look for edges, helping us to distinguish figure from background and consequently get our bearings . . ." (Pascale, Milleman, Gioja, 2000, p. 67)

Perhaps we often choose control over participation because the dynamic that is near the surface is more often fear than faith. Perhaps we haven't really understood the organic nature of the body. Perhaps we felt justified by scientific models that are now outdated.[25] Perhaps we just don't trust the Holy Spirit. Whatever the reason, coercion doesn't release creative people, it stifles them. If we want to increase ownership, and thus creativity, we are going to have to join the shift from consumers to producers, and that means empowering every member of the community.

Conclusion

With the close of the Modern Age the church became increasingly homogeneous, inward-oriented, and centralized in control. As a result, we lost touch with the biblical emphasis on community, participation, and the importance of context. As we moved broadly in North American churches into the reactive zone, we made it increasingly less likely that we would see an adaptive response to complex conditions.

But God isn't finished with us yet. There is experimentation going on at the edges. Many leaders have begun raising questions about the deep nature of the church and the need to rediscover a missional God. We have become aware of the tensions between design and emergence. We are admitting we are lost. Many are entering the space between recovering practices of Sabbath and silence. In this strange location, we find we need one another; traditional barriers between churches are breaking down. We are relearning how to be listeners and followers.

This journey is nearly complete. In the final chapter we'll talk about vocation, and the unusual demands of exile. We'll consider some

---

[25] Goodwin (1999) writes, "Scientific knowledge, originally seen to make possible the prediction and manipulation of nature, [is now] pointing us toward a new relationship with the natural world based on sensitive observation and **participation**, rather than **control**. That requires the cultivation of a new type of science, though its roots are already present in the old." [emphasis added]

questions about the engagement with mystery and beauty, those things that offer meaning and texture to our lives, and without which our lives become thin. Then I'll suggest some strategies for living on pilgrimage.

Love is most nearly itself
When here and now cease to matter.
Old men ought to be explorers
Here or there does not matter
We must be still and still moving
Into another intensity
For a further union, a deeper communion

(Eliot, 1960)

The severest test of work today is not of our strategies
but of our imaginations and identities.

(Whyte, 2001)

Chapter 7

Leadership in Exile

And so empires of ideas, as well as empires of wealth and power, come and go. To live well is to observe in today's apparent order the tiny anomalies that are the seeds of change, the harbingers of the order of tomorrow. This means living in a state of a certain insecurity, in anguish and loneliness, which, at its best, can push us toward the new. Too much security and the refusal to evolve, to embrace change, leads to a kind of death. Too much insecurity, however, can also mean death. To be human is to create sufficient order so that we can move on into insecurity and seeming disorder. In this way, we discover the new. (Vanier, 1998, p .13)

In chapter one we looked at the four phases of the adaptive cycle. The final phase was the renewal phase. Following a disturbance, uncertainty rules. Small, chance events have the opportunity to powerfully shape the future.

Stable systems are not lacking for change; but change is predictable. Discontinuous change is another animal. Sometimes we call this kind of change "phase transition." In discontinuous change, sudden shifts can happen that surprise us; structures that appear fixed and solid can collapse in a very short time.

185

With phase transition, a threshold is crossed; rather than more of the same occurring, something completely new happens. There's a sudden jump to a new state of reality. A solid becomes a liquid. Consider November 1989 when the Berlin Wall suddenly came down. We would think it impossible for water to break glass, but at a certain temperature ice forms and the seemingly impossible occurs.[26]

I find this encouraging when I remember the state of the church and discipleship and mission in the West. Change seems so slow – like molasses in winter. But we can't really measure the impact of small acts of faithfulness. We don't know the threshold. When we get close to it the smallest step may carry us over. When change finally occurs we probably won't know how or why.

Every time we take a small step forward, we can't measure how our movement will impact others. When one change makes the next more likely, or when strange attractors are in operation outside our field of vision, a cascade of events can lead to a breakthrough. Like a snowball rolling downhill, each moment adds energy.

In 1785 a Cambridge student named Thomas Clarkson entered an essay competition. The subject was slavery. As he began his research, his interest turned to horror. His essay won the prize, but he couldn't sleep. Abandoning his plans to become an Anglican minister, he joined a small group of Quakers who were working to shift public sentiment against slavery. Two years later he was one of a dozen people meeting in a London print shop who launched the Society for Effecting Abolition of the Slave Trade. The odds were stacked against them. It took Clarkson and fellow abolitionist William Wilberforce and their small society nearly twenty years, but inexorably the tide turned and the slave trade was ended.

---

[26] I'm reminded here of *Alice in Wonderland* and the Queen's response to Alice, "Why, sometimes I've believed as many as six impossible things before breakfast."

The End of Exile

"It is among exiles that Yahweh calls into existence things that do not exist" (Brueggemann, 1977, p. 3).

Peter wrote his letters to exiles, specifically to the "pilgrims in exile" (1 Pet 1:1). Like Walter Brueggemann in *Cadences of Home*, it's clear to Peter that living in exile is living in danger of loss of memory.

The theological metaphor of exile may help us to understand the cultural shift that is occurring, and the place of the church within it. Exile is not primarily geographical, but social, moral and cultural. Brueggemann notes that, "The exiled Jews of the OT were of course geographically displaced. More than that, however, the exiles experienced a loss of the structured, reliable world which gave them meaning and coherence, and they found themselves in a context where their most treasured and trusted symbols of faith were mocked, trivialized, or dismissed." (Brueggemann, 1997, p. 2)

Exile at first feels like abandonment, but it takes us to the place where we finally become useful to God. Bereft of our own adequacy, we must relearn a trust we thought we had never left. Exile comes to an end not when we are restored; not because we return home. As Lee Beach points out in his study, in diaspora there is no going home. (Beach, 2016). There is no path that will restore the church to the centre of our culture. But exile comes to its "end," its fruitful purpose, when we learn that God has been present with us in exile. We put our shoulders to the task not because we are guaranteed success, but because we are called. We need a fresh start, and we would not make one if our current structures were not collapsing.

My family and I have faced at least four major transitions in the past fifteen years. It's never easy. Transition invites us to embrace a new level of insecurity; each time it forces us to learn a new level of dependence on the Lord. Stepping into darkness is foolishness in the eyes of the world. No matter. We are working for a Master who weaves his faithful ways in hiddenness and mystery.

I will try
to fasten into order enlarging grasps of disorder, widening
scope, but enjoying the freedom that
Scope eludes my grasp, that there is not finality of vision,
that I have perceived nothing completely,
that tomorrow a new walk is a new walk.
"Corsons Inlet. " (A.R. Ammons, 2001)

One of the most beautiful stories in the gospels is the parable of the sower and the seed. (Matt 13.1-23) Paul picks up Jesus' metaphor when he recalls his own work: He planted, Apollos watered, and God gave the growth (1 Cor 3.6). The secret of waiting is faith. Growth is a mystery; it's not in our control. But the seed has been planted; something has begun. Active waiting means trusting in God's work, and being fully present in the moment. Something is happening right where you are. A waiting person believes that this moment is *the* moment. What prevents us from fully engaging in this moment is fear.

In *Active Hope* Chris Johnstone shares a story from a turning point in his life. (Macy & Johnstone, 2012, p. 231). After nearly ten years of medical training, he had resigned and was out of a job. It felt to him like a life-or-death decision. Just a few months before, while recovering from a working week of 112 hours, he had fallen asleep while driving and totaled his car. Now he sat on a hill in Wales, legs wobbly with fear, knees like jelly. As he sat there watching the clouds and the grass and listening to the chirp of crickets, suddenly he burst out laughing. He'd been hit by a moment of clarity – deep truth – and it seemed quite funny. His problem was fear: he didn't know what was going to happen. Yet it was the *not knowing* that made for mystery. He didn't know what lay around the corner, but the act of opening up to the mystery and adventure left him suddenly flush with expectation.

Perhaps as you finish this book you are still in a fearful space. There are many unknowns. You are caught between the world you knew and the unknown world of the future – a mystery. How will you stay grounded and open as you wait in this space between the two worlds? What might feel like a trap is not really a trap at all; it's a womb – a place of rebirth. In his middle years the poet Dante experienced something similar. He wrote,

> In the middle of the road of my life
> I woke in a dark wood
> where the way was truly lost. (Dante Aligheiri, 2012, p. 1)

The poet knows what it is to find himself off the map. It feels like darkness, not light. The way forward is not clear and there is no way back. We experience the tension between the known and the unknown. Our culture tells us that all our options should be laid out clearly, the possibilities displayed with little check boxes on a glowing screen. But life is not like that. The invisibles are as critical as the visibles.

Remember, you are not lost – *you're right here*. Our anxiety at the sensation of being lost is the problem, because it rouses the old brain and causes us to try harder, rather than to slow down and reflect. Overwhelmed by vague emotions, our brains stop working and we watch for the smallest signs that the landscape might somehow be familiar. We won't find those signs, because too much has changed. When we stop looking externally and turn inward, listening for the quiet voice of Love, hope and faith are renewed. Suddenly we claim the cage as a gift and it opens up into something else. Saying to ourselves, "Even this is enough" moves us beyond the trap.

What Is Essential

Antoine Marie Jean-Baptiste de Saint-Exupéry was a French writer, poet, aristocrat, journalist, and pioneering aviator. He was born in Lyon, France, on June 29, 1900. His father died when he was a young boy, and his mother moved him and his four siblings to a relative's château in the east. Antoine enjoyed a mostly carefree and privileged life, and in 1912 took his first trip in an airplane—an experience that would have a profound and lasting impression on him.

Receiving his early education at Catholic schools in France, Antoine was sent to a boarding school in Switzerland after the outbreak of World War I. He returned to France in 1917 and briefly attended a college prep school in Paris before attempting to enter the naval academy. However, Saint-Exupéry was a poor student; he failed the examination and studied architecture at the École des Beaux-Arts instead.

Despite his disappointing rejection from the naval academy, in 1921 Antoine de Saint-Exupéry was given the opportunity to realize his dreams of flying during his compulsory service in the military. While working as a mechanic in the army, he learned how to fly. He joined the air force the following year, and was based in North Africa. His engagement to a young woman resulted in his leaving the air force in 1922, but when their relationship failed he returned to his first love, flying, and developed a second passion—writing.

While working various jobs, Saint-Exupéry began to write stories inspired by his experiences as a pilot. He published his first work, "The Aviator," in 1926, the same year that he returned to flying as a mail pilot with Aéropostale in Toulouse. The remainder of his life would be defined by his dual loves of flight and literature.

In 1927, Saint-Exupéry was placed in charge of an airfield in the Sahara. His experiences there informed his first novel, *Southern Mail*, which celebrated the courage of pilots, was published in 1929. His similarly themed *Night Flight* was published in 1931 after he returned from a two-year posting in Argentina.

In 1931, Antoine de Saint-Exupéry married Salvadoran writer and artist Consuelo Suncin. Their marriage was not an easy one given Antoine's absences and infidelity. Among the most significant events was his 1935 attempt to break the air-speed record between Paris and Saigon. En route, his plane crashed in the Sahara, and he and his copilot wandered the desert for days, nearly dying of exposure and dehydration before being rescued by a wandering Bedouin. Saint-Exupéry's 1939 memoir *Wind, Sand and Stars*, won the prestigious Grand Prize for Novel Writing from the Académie Française and the National Book Award in the United States ("Antoine de Saint-Exupery," 2016).

But neither his growing literary success nor the disabilities resulting from several crashes stopped him from flying, and when World War II broke out he became a military reconnaissance pilot until the German occupation forced him to flee France for New York. It was while residing there that his most beautiful work was published: *The Little Prince*. The story is a fable for adults, and tells the mystical tale of a pilot stranded in the desert, and his conversation with a young prince from another planet. It was written and illustrated by Saint-Exupéry and published in both French and English in the United States in 1943.

The story begins with the narrator explaining his early attempts as an artist. He once drew a picture of a boa constrictor digesting an elephant; however, every adult who saw the picture mistakenly interpreted it as a drawing of a hat. Whenever he would try to correct this error, he was advised to set aside drawing and take up a more practical or mature hobby. The narrator laments the crass materialism of society, and the failure of imagination displayed by adults.

Now an adult himself, the narrator has become a pilot – a mature occupation! And one day, his plane crashes in the Sahara, far from civilization. Pondering his fate, he wakes one morning and sees a young boy. Confused in this space between, he is no less amazed when the boy asks him to draw a sheep. "When a mystery is too overpowering, one dare not disobey" (Saint-Exupéry, 2011). Still carrying his childhood sketching pad, the pilot first shows him his old picture of the elephant inside the snake, which, to his astonishment, the prince interprets correctly. He then proceeds to draw a realistic rendering of a sheep. After three failed attempts, the frustrated pilot simply draws a box, claiming that the box holds a sheep inside. To his surprise, the prince exclaims that this is *exactly* the picture he wanted.

The pilot and the prince share a number of experiences, but mostly the pilot listens as the little prince tells his stories. He left his small planet because something new happened: a rose bloomed and he fell in love with her. But she was demanding and vain, and the prince did not understand her. In his frustration, he knew he had to grow, and so he left his planet to travel. When he meets the pilot, he has already traveled widely on the earth, and has had significant encounters. He is learning just how complex it is to love. Once he met a fox and befriended him. But eventually the time came to say goodbye. As they part, the fox tells him a secret: "only with the heart can one see rightly; what is essential is invisible to the eye." (Saint-Exupéry, 2011).

What is essential is invisible to the eye. The demands of adulthood push us into a pragmatic world, where we become focused on "bottom lines," and our inner life shrivels. We become enamored with the upward journey, and with the tokens of success. We become service providers and lose our sense of pilgrimage, and the importance of love and beauty. Inevitably, we then become task masters, pushing others to achievements that will in turn reflect on our own ability as leaders. In doing so we insulate others from their own joy and passion. Saint-Exupéry offers an alternative: "If you want to build a ship, don't drum up people to collect wood and then assign them tasks and work, but rather teach them to yearn for the endless sea." (Saint-Exupéry, 2003 p. 43).

Love, beauty, mystery: things we both fear and yearn for. These qualities often come to us as a gift; they appear in our lives uninvited. Like Chris Johnstone sitting on the hill engulfed in fear: suddenly a new vista opens before us. The journey that prepares us for these things is rarely one we choose. Rather, we encounter these qualities in liminal spaces, when they are beyond our grasp.

In *Falling Upward* Richard Rohr speaks of the necessity of a new orientation for the second half of one's life, and warns that most churches do not know how to make room for the tasks that lie ahead. They do not know how to include the reality of tragedy, and they offer no rituals for the passage from life's first half to the second. Instead, they remain focused on progress, success, and youth. Yet all the classical heroes -- Odysseus, Hercules, Orpheus, Psyche – descended to the realms of the dead before rising again. Jesus' path was first one of descent: incarnation, rejection, and death. And while Jonah didn't make that kind of descent, his three days in the belly of the whale are offered by Jesus as a foretelling of the kind of journey he himself must make. Carl Jung writes, "One cannot live the afternoon of life according to the program of life's morning; for what was great in the morning will be of little importance in the evening, and what in the morning was true will at evening have become a lie" (Jung, Fordham, & Adler, 1953).

Living Among Exiles

It is among exiles that Yahweh calls into existence things that do not exist.[27]

The problem I have been addressing in these seven chapters was not actually the problem of a complex culture, or the problem of non-adaptive solutions, or our inability to welcome change, serious as these issues are. The problem I have been addressing, albeit indirectly, is the loss of a spiritual center. It's true that we need new leadership paradigms, and we need to understand the new context we are living in. But these things won't help us move forward if we aren't renewed in our souls. As Augustine writes in his *Confessions*, "How can you draw close to God when you are far from your own self?" The call is to pay attention to deep self.

It's nearly a cliché that our culture is addicted to climbing the ladder. In chapter 3 we considered the fitness landscape, moving down

---

[27] Brueggemann, *The Land*, 117

to move up. Then we discussed the paradox of ascent. Our image of success is a linear upward movement, growing our careers and our bank accounts so that we can holiday in a tropical climate, drinking margaritas with our friends. Even the language most basic to maturity describes our bias: life is about *growing up.*

But life is not all about growing up. Any tree that stands is alternately dancing between its reach upward to the light, and its reach down into the soil. In the warm and wet weather, trees expand their reach upward; the rest of the year is consolidation, getting a grip on the earth. When our accustomed upward movement is blocked, the invitation is to grow deeper. Our rational mind balks at the call; but our soul yearns to listen. Robert Browning, in his classic poem, describes the paradox:

> Rejoice we are allied
> To That which doth provide
> And not partake, effect and not receive!
> A spark disturbs our clod;
> Nearer we hold of God
> Who gives, than of His tribes that take, I must believe.
>
> Then, welcome each rebuff
> That turns earth's smoothness rough,
> Each sting that bids nor sit nor stand but go!
> Be our joys three-parts pain!
> Strive, and hold cheap the strain;
> Learn, nor account the pang; dare, never grudge the throe!
>
> For thence,—a paradox
> Which comforts while it mocks,—
> Shall life succeed in that it seems to fail:
> What I aspired to be,
> And was not, comforts me:

A brute I might have been, but would not sink i' the scale.[28]

"What I aspired to be, and was not, comforts me." Browning is talking about the call of the soul, the inner voice that demands recognition. The old Latin word for voice is "vocare," from which we derive vocation. Each one of us responds to an inner call, and woe to us if we avoid the call! Our soul will not rest easy, and will buck and kick and scream until we take notice. There are necessities we can avoid for a time, but the necessities of soul will not be evaded. The Welsh poet David Whyte says, "If you can see the path laid out before you, chances are it's not your path but someone else's you have substituted for your own."[29]

We all face a choice: we can be managers or mystics. The mystic vocation is to unite vocation and work: to respond to the inner call to become what God has made us to be. That call is written deep in the fabric of our being. Our first and greatest task, beyond our career, beyond the applause of the crowd or the approval of our superiors, is the call to become our true selves. Inevitably, this is a lonely path, a path familiar to exiles.

Loneliness is a fact of human existence. We experience it commonly as a response to personal tragedy. Waves of loneliness hit us as aftershocks of relational car-wrecks, the death of someone we loved, the sudden loss of a job. To guard against the pain we have philosophies to explain it and drugs to deny it. Loneliness is a symptom of victimization, the depersonalization of work, a result of a harried existence. We should not be lonely. The system is broken. Pick up the phone and connect; get a prescription for Prozac.

But loneliness is more than existential or a result of circumstance; it comes and goes without apparent cause. At its root it is

---

[28] Robert Browning, "Rabbi Ben Ezra"

[29] David Whyte, *The Heart Aroused* (New York: Doubleday, 1994)

a yearning for something outside this world, something we can connect with only partially. Living your life requires above all time, a lot of it. But the digital world truncates time, and the demands of ailing institutions demand more and more of our limited store. When life is rushed it becomes an abstract package, devoid of meaning. You can no longer offer yourself to the present moment. At the tempo of modernity everything becomes thin, until you are absent from your own life.

The best connection is participation; finding our unique voice and expressing it in the world. That expression will always be a struggle, because a myriad of external voices will try to tell us who we are. Always there is someone who thinks they know us better than we know ourselves. Creatives and visionaries experience loneliness more often that the rest because they are continually venturing where no one has gone before. It looks like foolishness to the crowd. Why take the risk when the well-worn path invites? Responding to the inner voice is thus a lonely task, and requires us to become pilgrims.

Becoming the Pilgrim

Pilgrimage is an old practice – possibly older than Christianity itself. As a practice it is enjoying a remarkable recovery: witness the number of people who take the road on the Camino de Santiago each year. Why the renaissance? Very likely because the times are demanding more of us than we can give. We are forced to recover an inward journey.

But an inward journey is not enough for the body. The requirements of the soul include enfleshment, so we put our feet on the path and start walking. But where are we going? What is this journey about?

Crucially, the poets are out there ahead of us, moving their feet along with us. A number of current songs deal with the realities of pilgrimage. In chapter 2 I referenced *Pacing the Cage.* Here is another citation –

I've proven who I am so many times
The magnetic strip's worn thin
And each time I was someone else
And every one was taken in
Hours chatter in high places
Stir up eddies in the dust of rage
Set me to pacing the cage[30]

The soul will never be satisfied with outward clothing that fails to match inward realities. We yearn for something we have not seen. It's the lesson of 1 Samuel 17 – Saul's armor doesn't fit the future king David. He must find his own way to defeat the giant. Unless he does, the inner response will be rage and then a depression that will consume him. Similarly, the journey from where we are to where we must go will be unique to our soul.

Another poet describes the journey of the Magi in terms that reflect the demands of the mystery. Steve Bell and Jamie Howison write of the surrender such a commitment requires.

So we set off for a foreign land
With no idea what we just might find
'cause when you're following a star
You have to walk at night
Sounds crazy even now

When you are truly on your own road the journey includes both light and darkness. It's disorienting; the kind of lostness experienced in mountain fog. Your good friends will tell you you're crazy! And because it requires leaving familiar places behind, it results in the kind of inner

---

[30] Bruce Cockburn, "Pacing the Cage." From *The Charity of Night*, 1995. Golden Mountain Music Corporation. BMI.

change that makes any return impossible. In a sense we can never go home again.

> And still the search goes on for
> My way back home
> I can't go back the way I've known
> And now the road for me has changed
> Nothing seems to look the same
> Don't get me wrong I'm not complaining[31]

The road changes us; nothing looks the same. And while there may eventually be some sense of arrival, the journey teaches us that we are never completely at home in this world. We long to be fully present with the One who loves us completely. We yearn for a future marriage, a deeper fulfilment.

Yet the qualities of pilgrimage and the richness of the experience are not reserved only for those who board a plane for Spain. In every location of life, we put our feet on the road with a yearning for something more. We follow the star in every location of life.

Consequently pilgrimage is a study in itself, and it will be helpful for some to discern its structure. The classic stages of pilgrimage are six:

1. Yearning
2. Preparation
3. The Journey / Disorientation
4. Approaching / Arriving
5. The Sacred Experience
6. The Return

Stage 1. You find yourself yearning for something you have not known. Pascal wrote in his *Pensées*: "the heart has its reasons that reason

---

[31] Old Sage. *The Feast of Seasons*. Winnipeg, MB. Signpost Music, 1995.

cannot know." The yearning leads you to search, and to begin to let go of familiar territory. What you are and where you are is no longer enough.

Preparation is the next phase. You begin an internal waiting, and listening with an expectancy you have not previously known. Charles Foster comments that, "What sets the pilgrim apart [from the tourist] is that he hopes, and at some level believes, that someone will hear his footsteps coming from afar ... and that from inside will come music that he has heard somewhere before." (Sacred Journey, 109)

Next comes the Journey; walking the path. This is the actual transition, the in-between space. There is a sense of disorientation. It's an immersive, absorbing place. At this stage we usually look for companions and guides. If we are truly blessed, we find them. Sometimes there is a sense of losing yourself and losing the role of observer. "We are pilgrims on the earth and strangers; "we have come from afar and we are going far."[32]

Next is Approaching and arriving. This is re-orientation. This is a great moment, when you see, however distant, the goal of your wandering. "The thing which has been living in your imagination suddenly becomes a part of the tangible world." - Freya Stark (b. 1983, British explorer)

And if you haven't made the connection yet, this is all about the life that we live. Pilgrimage – if you are a follower of Jesus – is where you are every day. Pilgrimage is the practice of attention in an open space. If you left pilgrimage behind, chances are that you stopped actively following Jesus. And now you have to find your life before you can lose it.

The fifth stage is the Sacred Experience. Something in you has changed – it may take time to sort out what it is. Perhaps you lack

---

[*] Attributed to Vincent van Gogh

language for it. It feels paradoxical: like knowing and not knowing at the same time. "The more you see, the less you know / the less you find out as you go / I knew much more then, than I do now."[33]

Finally comes the Return. "Old things have passed away, all things become new." In the end is our beginning. The return is truly an invitation to begin again. Anglican poet Malcolm Guite advises us to begin where we are.

> Begin the song exactly where you are,
> Remain within the world of which you're made.
> Call nothing common in the earth or air,
> Accept it all and let it be for good.
> Start with the very breath you breathe in now,
> This moment's pulse, this rhythm in your blood
> And listen to it, ringing soft and low.
> Stay with the music, words will come in time.
> Slow down your breathing. Keep it deep and slow.
> Become an open singing-bowl, whose chime
> Is richness rising out of emptiness,
> And timelessness resounding into time.
> And when the heart is full of quietness
> Begin the song exactly where you are.[34]

<small>33</small> U2 "City of Blinding Lights"

<small>34</small> Malcolm Guite, *The Singing Bowl* (Norwich: Canterbury Press, 2013)

Coda

A friend's email arrived a moment ago with the familiar "beep" and I opened his note to read a reference to "the death of workshops." Until recently there was a workshop or seminar for everything. Those of us who lead and who teach are overwhelmed with information. How do we sort through it all to find the stuff that is really useful?

If you picked up this book, it's likely because the title reflected something of your own soul. You may feel a measure of desperation. Or, perhaps you work with leaders and you are watching for resources that can help. No matter. If you made it this far, there must have been something worthwhile here. I'm honored. I walked with you a short time, and now I have to wish you Godspeed on your journey. What closing thought can I offer? What can I say that hasn't been said?

My parting wish is that you will find partners on your journey. I promise you won't regret that decision! We need friends who will walk with us through liminal spaces; they will offer support and encouragement and needed perspective. They will have clarity or at least sympathy when we need it the most. They'll help us get beyond the ego focus that so often results when we feel stuck. And they'll keep us honest.

But there is another reason that pilgrim partners or soul friends are so important, and it's that they will help us discern the signs of newness before we are able to see them ourselves. And when we need the courage to launch down a new road, they'll offer us their own strength. The truth is that we rarely go to new places alone. And as our African friends say, "If you want to go fast, go alone. If you want to go far, go together."

Godspeed!

About the Author

Len Hjalmarson is the author of *The Missional Church Fieldbook* and co-author, with Roger Holland, of *Missional Spirituality* (IVP: 2011). In 2014, he published *No Home Like Place: A Christian Theology of Place* (ULP), which won the Grace Irwin Prize and best in Academic category at the Word Guild. Len lives with his wife Betty in North Ontario where they pastor a community together. Len is a member of the Parish Collective.

Len holds a doctorate from ACTS in Langley, BC, and is an adjunct professor at Tyndale Seminary, Toronto and at Portland Seminary where he is an advisor in the Leadership in Global Perspectives program. He is a founding member of the North Ontario Theological Association (NOTA). When not teaching or writing, he can be found trying to perfect his bread recipe, reading science fiction, or hiking around the hills near his home.

References

A & E Television Networks. (2016). *Antoine de Saint-Exupery.* Retrieved from
      http://www.biography.com/people/antoine-de-saint-exupery-030816

Alves, Rubem A. (1990). *The poet, the warrior, the prophet.* London: SCM Press.

Ammons, A.R. (2001) Collected Poems: 1951-1971. WW Norton.

Augustine. (1998). *The confessions* (M. Boulding, Trans.). New York: Vintage
      Books.

Bauman, Zygmunt. (2000). *Liquid Modernity.* Cambridge: Polity.

Barth, Karl. (1959). *Dogmatics in Outline.* New York: Harper Perennial.

Barton, Ruth Haley. (2011). Pursuing God's Will Together. Downer's Grove:
      IVP.

Beach, Lee. (2016). *The Church in Exile: Living in Hope After Christendom.*
      Downer's Grove: IVP.

Berry, Wendell. (1998) *A Timbered Choir.* Washington: Counterpoint.

Block, Peter. (2009). *Community: The Structure of Belonging.* San Francisco:
      Berrett-Koehler.

Bosch., David. (1991).*Transforming Mission: Paradigm Shifts in Theology of Mission.*
      Orbis Books.

Brafman, Ori & Beckstrom, R. (2006). *The Starfish and the Spider: The
      Unstoppable Power of Leaderless Organizations.* New York: Penguin
      Group.

Brandt, Gareth. (2014). *Spirituality with Clothes On.* Eugene: Wipf & Stock.

Brannen, Peter. (2016, Sept. 20). The Last Great Arctic Shipwreck. *The Atlantic
      Monthly.* Retrieved from
      http://www.theatlantic.com/science/archive/2016/09/northwest-
      passage/500753/

Brewin, Kester. (2007). *Signs of Emergence.* Grand Rapids: Baker Books.

Browning, Robert. (1995). *Robert Browning: Selected Poems.* New York:
      Blackstone.

Brueggemann, Walter. (1977). *The Land.* Philadelphia: Fortress Press.

Brueggemann, Walter. (1997). *Cadences of Home: Preaching Among Exiles.*
      Louisville: Westminster John Knox Press.

_____. (2001). *Spirituality of the Psalms*. Minneapolis: Augsburg Fortress.

Buker, Bill. (2003). Spiritual Development and the Epistemology of Systems Theory. *Journal of Psychology and Theology*. 31(2). 148.

Capra, Fritjof. (1983). *The Turning Point*. New York: Bantam Books.

_____. (2002).*The Hidden Connections*. New York: Anchor Books.

Clairvaux, B. (1983). *On loving God* (S. Tompkins, Trans.). New York: HarperCollins.

Clear, James. (2012, November). "Successful People Start Before They Feel Ready." Retrieved from http://jamesclear.com/successful-people-start-before-they-feel-ready

Cleveland, Harlan. (2002). *Nobody in Charge*. San Francisco: Jossey-Bass.

Cloud, Henry. (2010). *Necessary Endings*. New York: HarperCollins.

Bruce Cockburn, "Pacing the Cage." From *The Charity of Night*, 1995. Golden Mountain Music Corporation. BMI.

Dante Alighieri. (2012) *La Divine Commedia*. Amazon Digital Services.

De la Crux, S., & Nims, J. F. (1979). *The poems of St. John of the Cross*. Chicago: University of Chicago.

Jacques Derrida, *Différance* (Paris: Editions Seuil, 1968)

Eliot, T.S. (1960). *Four Quartets*. London: Faber & Faber.

_____. (1990). Choruses from 'The Rock.' *Collected Poems: 1909 to 1962*. London: Faber & Faber.

Finkel, Michael. (2000, May). "Someone There is Who Loves a Wall." *The Atlantic Monthly*. Retrieved from https://www.theatlantic.com/magazine/archive/2000/05/someone-there-is-who-loves-a-wall/378213/

Foster, Charles. (2010). *The Sacred Journey*. Nashville: Thomas Nelson. Friesen, D. (2005, June 5). Networks and leadership. Retrieved July 8, 2005, from http://dwightfriesen.blog.com

Gibbs, Eddie. (2005). *Leadership Next*. Downer's Grove: IVP.

Goldman, Eric.(2007, Jan. 16) How Will Lost End? Retrieved from http://tv.ign.com/articles/755/755527p2.html

Gonzales, Laurence. (2003). *Deep Survival: Who Lives, Who Dies and Why*. New York: WW Norton & Company.

Goodwin, Brian. (1999. Spring). From Control to Participation via a Science of Qualities. *ReVision*, 21(4).

Guite, Malcolm. (2013). *The Singing Bowl.* Norwich: Canterbury Press.

Gunderson, Lance H. (2012). *Panarchy: Understanding Transformations in Human and Natural Systems.* [Kindle Edition]. Island Press.

Hagberg, Janet and Guelich, R. (2005). *The Critical Journey.* New York: Sheffield Publishing.

Hastings, Ross. (2012. Nov. 6). Identity in a Missional God. Retrieved from http://onlinepulpit.ivpress.com/2012/11/identity_in_a_missional_god.php

Heifetz, Ron. (1994). *Leadership Without Easy Answers.* Harvard University Press.

Hesselbein, Frances. *Hesselbein on Leadership.* San Francisco: Jossey-Bass.

Hippel, Eric Von. (2005). *Democratizing Innovation.* MIT Press.

Hlatshwayo, Godwin. (2008). Quoted in Block, Peter. *Community: The Structure of Belonging.* San Francisco: Berret-Koehler Publishers.

Hoffer, Eric. (1969). *Working and Thinking on the Waterfront.* New York: Harper & Row.

Homer-Dixon, Thomas. (2007). *The Upside of Down.* Toronto: Vintage Canada.

Jamieson, Alan. (2000). *A Churchless Faith.* Auckland: Philip Garside Publishing.

Johnson, Steven. (2002). *Emergence: The Connected Lives of Ants, Brains, Cities and Software.* New York: Scribner

Jung, C. G. (1953). *The collected works of C. G. Jung* (Vol. 8) (M. S. Fordham, Ed.; G. Adler, Trans.). New York: Pantheon Books.

Jung, Carl. (1992). Letters, Volume I. Princeton University Press.

Kelly, Kevin. (1997, September) New Rules for the New Economy. *Wired Magazine.*

Kilpatrick, Sue and Falk, I. and Johns, S. (1998). Leadership in Dynamic Learning Communities. Tasmania: University of Tasmania.

Kinnaman, David. (2011). *You Lost Me.* Grand Rapids: Baker Books.

Leclercq, Jean. (1982) *The Love of Learning and the Desire for God.* New York: Fordham University Press.

Longfellow, H. W. (2012). *The complete poetical works of Henry Wadsworth Longfellow.* Dayboro: Emereo Pub.

Lowry, Eugene. (2000).*The Homiletical Plot.* Louisville: Westminster John Knox Press.

Mcluhan, Marshall and Fiore, Q. (2001). *The Medium is the Message.* Corte Madera, CA: Gingko.

McNeal, Reggie. (2000). *A Work of Heart.* San Francisco: Jossey-Bass.
_____. (2003). *The Present Future.* San Francisco: Jossey-Bass.
Mayer, Peter. (2001). "Fall." *Million Year Mind.* New Jersey: Home Town Music.
Meadows, Donella. (1982, Summer). Whole Earth Models and Systems. Co-Evolution Quarterly.
Miller, Lawrence. (1990). *Barbarians to Bureaucrats: Corporate Life Cycle Strategies.* New York: Clarkson-Potter.
Morgenthaler, Sally. (2007). Leadership in a Flattened World," in *An Emergent Manifesto of Hope.* Grand Rapids: Baker Books.
Morse, Marykate. (2012). *The Gospel After Christendom*, Ryan K. Bolger, ed. Grand Rapids: Baker Academic.
Myers, Joseph R. (2003). *The Search to Belong*. Grand Rapids, MI: Zondervan.
Neave, Rosemary. (1996). "Reimagining the Church," Women's Resource Center, NZ. Study Report Leave.
Newbigin, Lesslie. (1981). *Sign of the Kingdom.* Grand Rapids: Wm B. Eerdmans.
Nouwen, Henri. (1981). *The Way of the Heart.* New York: HarperCollins.
Nouwen, Henri. (1983). *The Genesee Diary.* New York: Bantam Dell Publishing.
_____. (1996) *Bread for the Journey: A Daybook of Wisdom and Faith*. New York: HarperOne.
Palmer, Parker J. (2000). *Let Your Life Speak: Listening for the Voice of Vocation.* San Francisco: Jossey-Bass.
Parks, Sharon Daloz. (2007, November) The Undergraduate Quest for Meaning, Purpose and Faith. *Spirituality in Higher Education.* 4(1).
_____. (1999). *Big Questions, Worthy Dreams.* San Francisco: Jossey-Bass.
Pascale, R. T., Millemann, M. & Gioja, L. (2000). *Surfing the Edge of Chaos.* New York: Three Rivers Press.
Peterson, Eugene. (1989). *The Contemplative Pastor.* Grand Rapids: Wm. B. Eerdmans.
Plowman, D.A., Solansky, S., Beck, T.E., Baker, L., Kulkarni, M. & Travis, D.V. (2007). The role of leadership in emergent selforganization. *The Leadership Quarterly* 18(4), 341–356.
Potok, Chaim. (2001). *My First 79 Years: Isaac Stern.* New York: Da Capo Press.
Ramo, Joshua Cooper. (2009). *The Age of the Unthinkable.* New York: Back Bay Books.

Rilke, R. M. (1981). *Selected poems of Rainer Maria Rilke* (R. Bly, Trans.). New York: Harper.

Rohr, Richard. (2002, February) Days Without Answers in a Narrow Space. *National Catholic Reporter.*

Roxburgh, Alan J. (1997). *The Missionary Congregation, Leadership & Liminality.* Harrisburg, Pennsylvania: Trinity Press International.

_____. (2005). *The Sky is Falling: Leaders Lost in Transition.* Eagle, ID: ACI Publishing.

_____. (2008). Derivatives With A Twist. Retrieved from http://www.alanroxburgh.net/

_____. (2010), *Missional Map-Making.* San Francisco: Jossey Bass.

Roxburgh, Alan J. & Romanuk, Fred. (2006). *The Missional Leader.* San Francisco, CA: Jossey-Bass.

Rūmī, J. A. (2004). *The essential Rumi* (C. Barks, Trans.). New York: HarperCollins.

Saint-Exupéry, Antoine. (2011). *The Little Prince.* Numitor Comun Publishing.

_____. (2003). *The Wisdom of the Sands.* Amereon Limited.

Santmire, H. Paul. (1985). *The Travail of Nature: The Ambiguous Ecological Promise of Christian Theology.* Minneapolis: Fortress Press.

Saul, John Ralston. (2014). *The Comeback.* Toronto: Penguin Books.

Sedmak. Clemens. (2002). *Doing Local Theology: A Guide for Artisans of a New Humanity.* New York: Orbis Books.

Senge, *Peter.* (1990). *The Fifth Discipline: The Art and Practice of the Learning Organization.* Crown Books.

Senge, Peter, and Scharmer, C. O., and Jaworski, J. & Flowers, B. (2005). *Presence: An Exploration of Profound Change in People, Organizations and Society.* New York: Random House.

Simon & Garfunkel. (1966). "The 59th Street Bridge Song (Feeling Groovy)." On *Parsley, Sage, Rosemary and Thyme.* New York: Columbia Records.

Snyder, Howard. (1983). *Liberating the Church: The Ecology of Church and Kingdom.* Downer's Grove: IVP.

Sparks, Paul, and Soerens, T. & Friesen, D. (2014). *The New Parish.* Downer's Grove: IVP.

Spears, Larry. (2002). The Servant-Leader: from hero to host. Indianapolis: The Greenleaf Centre for Servant Leadership.

Stark, Freya. (2010). *A Winter in Arabia.* Tauris Parke Paperbacks.

Stevens, R. Paul. (1997) *The Other Six Days.* Grand Rapids: Eerdmans.

Syrotuck, William. (2000). *An Analysis of Lost Person Behavior.* Mechanicsburg, PA: Barkleigh Productions.

Sweet, Leonard. (2004). *Summoned to Lead.* Grand Rapids: Zondervan.

The Legend of Baggar Vance. (2000). Los Angeles: Allied Filmworkers.

U2. (2004). "City of Blinding Lights." From *How to dismantle an atom bomb.* Dublin: Island Music.

Van Gelder, Craig & Zscheile, D.J. (2011) *The Missional Church in Perspective.* Grand Rapids: Baker Books.

Vanier, Jean. (1989). *Community and Growth.* New York, NY: Paulist Press.

_____. (1998). *Becoming Human.* New York: Paulist Press.

Virilio, Paul and Oliveira, C. (1996, June 12). Global Algorithm 1.7: The Silence of the Lambs: Paul Virilio in Conversation. In: Patrice Rimens (Translator). *Ctheory.*

Waldrop, M. Mitchell. (1992). *Complexity.* Toronto: Touchstone Books.

Westley, Frances, and ZimmermanB. & Patton, M. (2006). Frances et al. *Getting to Maybe: How the World is Changed..* Toronto: Vintage Canada

What Reveal Reveals. (2008, February 27) *Christianity Today.* Retrieved from http://www.christianitytoday.com/ct/2008/march/11.27.html

Wheatley, Margaret. (1997, July). Goodbye Command and Control. *Leader to Leader.* No. 7.

_____. (1996, July). The Irresistible Future of Organizing.

_____. (1999. Winter). When Complex Systems Fail. *Leader to Leader.* No. 11.

_____. (2005). *Finding Our Way.* San Francisco: Berrett-Koehler.

White, Eric. (2007) A Passage Toward the Other: The Legacy of Jacques Derrida (1930-2004). The European Legacy. 12(4) 407-407.

Whyte, David. (2001). *Crossing the Unknown Sea.* New York: Riverhead Books.

_____. (2002). *The Heart Aroused.* New York: Doubleday.

Wright, Ronald. (2004). *A Short History of Progress.* Canada Council for the Arts.